Persuasion Tactics

Covert Psychology Strategies to Influence, Persuade, & Get Your Way

(Without Manipulation)

By Patrick King
Social Interaction Specialist and Social Skills
Coach at www.PatrickKingConsulting.com

Introduction

When I was in third grade, a fitness craze swept the nation.

In hindsight, it must have been related to the appointment of Arnold Schwarzenegger to the President's Council on Fitness, and the country was overly excited to have *the Terminator* in a position of actual authority. Of course, this was before the Terminator became the Governator of California, but I digress.

The reason I remember this so vividly was because my third grade teacher wholeheartedly embraced the fitness craze and had our entire class run a mile (1.6 kilometers) every day for a period of three months.

Corralling 30 hyper, obnoxious, and unofficially ADHD-diagnosed eight-year olds was a tall order, especially for a purpose that we had no concept of. Fitness to us as children was as abstract as a home mortgage, and we cared just as much about it.

Leading a class of children to a hot track on days where it was up to 90 degrees Fahrenheit (32 degrees Celsius) could take some serious pleading, and in fact I do remember some pleading on her behalf for the first few days.

Kids, not unlike adults, rarely react well to direct and forced persuasion. We'll go along grumbling and dragging our feet if we're commanded to do something, but sweetening the goal with other incentives is how society actually functions. In other words, finding motivation was key, lest my class unintentionally reenact *Lord of the Flies*.

It became quickly clear to my teacher that we needed motivation through something that wasn't fitness-related, so she issued us a challenge from a *fourth grade* class, who claimed that they could collectively improve their average mile time more than we could.

The stakes were high: the class with the most improved average time would have a pizza party thrown in their honor, complete with orange slices and soda.

Now that's motivation for an eight-year old!

The pizza party was actually secondary to our desire to take down some older kids. Suddenly running became a hobby to all of us, even to Big Bobby, as we called him, who had to walk most of the time.

We grew to love our daily mile, and *that's* how my third grade teacher was the first example of great persuasion I've seen in my life.

She was able to inspire us to action – an action which objectively is pretty terrible on a daily basis. But by indirectly avoiding the reality of running a mile in 90-degree heat, she changed the frame and made it about accepting a monumental challenge (remember, beating a fourth grader is a big deal for a third grader), coming together as a class, working towards a common reward, and fighting for our pride.

That's the most effective manner of persuasion – the kind where you can spur into people action by zeroing in on what drives people, what they want to avoid, and what will make them happy.

The vast majority of the time, what you want isn't quite what others will want. In essence, you will constantly be trying to lead people to contested and unpopular decisions. There will almost always be opposition to what you propose, and it's not your fault – people come into situations with their own preconceptions, notions, and baggage, so it's inevitable. But that doesn't change your overall objective of persuasion.

What do you do if the front door is barricaded? You find your way in through the windows and backdoor, and infiltrate the chimney.

In other words, you find a way to open the cracks of people's psychology to find exactly what drives them, and use that to inspire action and accomplish your objective. You find persuasion tactics to draw people in, make them think differently, and ultimately see your way.

That's the root of persuasion – realizing that most situations simply call for a smarter, more analytical approach, as opposed to bluster and bravado. Understanding that there are different types of people and motivation is key, but so are specific phrases and knowing how to capitalize on emotional decisions.

This isn't a book about techniques to magically make someone follow you to the ends of the earth – it's a book about *human engineering* and how to take advantage of the way people think and *tend* to think. When you know how someone thinks and what drives them, you can create a path that appeals to them.

I later found out that my teacher made the entire challenge up, but I couldn't help but commend her genius on how to keep a group of kids docile and generally easy to manage.

We still got our pizza party, and I learned a valuable lesson that children and adults alike are all ruled by the same basic desires that make persuasion tactics possible.

Chapter 1. The Butterfly Effect

Not all of us are born to be world-bending persuaders and influencers, but that isn't the worst thing in the world.

Most of us don't aspire to be Winston Churchill, nor do we need to. But that doesn't mean that we can't pick up skills along the way that will get us where we want to be, and produce the results that we want with the people around us.

Every single charismatic influencer that you feel compelled to follow – they were created in the sense that they've been highly trained on how to lead and persuade others to follow.

The real world has very little relationship to what our formal schooling prepared us for. You can learn geometry, or the capitals of countries, but when in your adult life will knowing those things put you where you want to be? Learning how to deal with people effectively is what will earn you the trust and respect that will make a positive difference in your daily life. And if you ever find yourself in a position of power, dealing effectively with people below you will be paramount for keeping that position!

What happens if you're in a leadership position and you can't persuade others to follow you?

Anarchy would be the expectation. You will also see a combination of resentment, bitterness, lack of accountability, lack of productivity, and overall malaise among those you are supposed to lead. Departments and employees may function well independently, but without strong coordination and sense of purpose, they can end up acting against each other. This situation can literally destroy companies and friendships.

leadership = persuasion

Even outside the context of work and hierarchical constructs, the personal traits of being able to persuade, lead, and influence are essential.

What kind of friend are you if your friends don't feel as if they can trust you, and you can't persuade them of anything? You will essentially be a pushover and doormat whom no one listens to. Others won't feel sure that you mean what you say, and that's an unsettling feeling.

Persuading and influencing isn't just about moving up the corporate ladder. Being a capable persuader can impact how much appeal you have to members of the opposite sex, the price you pay for things, how close your family is and, yes, your access to better jobs and opportunities.

It also impacts how others perceive you. Many people float through their days on cruise control, rarely thinking about breaking their routine or reaching for more. Deep down, most people are looking for people to follow and take cues from. If you are persuasive, people will feel compelled to follow you.

Who were Martin Luther and Martin Luther King, Jr. without their abilities to persuade and draw others to their cause?

The former would have just been a disgruntled priest who, in 1517, nailed a list of 95 demands to a church door. He had some complaints about the Roman Catholic Church that he chose to publicly air; if he hadn't been a compelling, passionate leader, his list of demands would probably have been tossed aside—along with his head. But, because of his leadership qualities and his ability to persuade others, he inspired a historical split in the Catholic Church.

The latter would have just been a minister who recognized racial inequality in the United States and didn't like it. Surely there were thousands of others who saw the same injustices and felt the same way, but none of *them* were able to lead hundreds of thousands of people in protest marches and launch an entire movement.

In other words, without their persuasive qualities, neither of these now famous men would have been more than historical footnotes. Without their ability to inspire others to follow them, their dreams would not have been realized.

When you look at people's lives and pay attention to what quality they have that allows them to achieve high levels of effectiveness, you will find that their ability to persuade others plays a prominent role.

Your ability to persuade and build trust impacts the quality of your life. The more trustworthy you are, the more people will willingly follow you. Building trust and the ability to persuade because of that trust is one of the greatest gateway traits you can possess – it's right up there with confidence (or an incredibly large bank account).

Being a gateway trait not only has its own value, but it derives value from the behaviors it generates.

When you inspire people to follow your lead, more gets done. It doesn't matter if your goal is to create a media empire, or just figure which restaurant to eat in.

The ability to gather people together to achieve a common goal (or *your* goal) is what has taken us from a loose gathering of hunter-gatherer tribes to the melting pot of cultures we are today. It's the difference between starting a revolution and creating action, and sitting around in your underwear talking about what you *would* do.

Persuasion is the spearhead to any action, large or small.

You don't lead because you have a badge or title; you lead because you can persuade others and draw them to your cause.

Chapter 2. Understand Your Actual Audience

I used to be a cat person.

That's right, those moody ankle-scratchers used to be my idea of a loyal and wonderful companion. Then I began dating someone who had a fluffy little Shih-Tzu – a dog that is considered by very masculine men to be... negligible.

But it turns out it's nice to be greeted at the door by a pet that not only acknowledges your existence, but craves your attention and presence. I'm now a dog person. It's not a stance that I will likely change now that I've seen both sides of the coin.

Many people have tried to convince me of the virtues of cats, but the fact is, they are wasting their time and effort. I've seen both sides of the coin, and I can rely on my experience to inform my choice. I'm not on fence.

The lesson is that some people just can't be persuaded away from their own perspective, no matter what you say or evidence you present to the contrary. They might be stubborn, set in their ways, close-minded, or all three, but you won't be able to persuade them to change their opinion.

Just getting better at persuasion and influencing does **not** mean you can convert or lead anyone. And that's okay because it just informs where you should spend your time and effort – focus your efforts on the persuadable!

Focus On The Persuadable

Some think that persuasion means the ability to transform anyone into a follower and overcome any objection. Those people are confusing leadership with mind control, hypnosis, and maybe a little bit too much *Star Wars*. Outside of physically or financially threatening someone, innate objections will always inform someone's choices.

The reality is that your persuasion skills will only work on people who are either (1) on the fence or (2) open to being persuaded. It will never work on people who have already made up their minds.

Of course, we should always start with the premise that everyone *is* on the fence and that everyone has an open mind you can engage to lead and persuade them.

But, if after you've spent a reasonable amount of effort you are still meeting with resistance and they aren't budging, then it's time to cut your losses and move on in the interest of efficiency and not wasting your time.

Part of the purpose of this chapter is to condition and

prepare you for inevitable rejection. Just as I'd rather own a dog over a cat, some people will simply reject your persuasive attempts for their own reasons. It's just the cost of standing up and trying something!

And that's okay.

Not Everyone Will Love You

Whenever you are addressing people, there will always be a percentage that you cannot reach. No matter what you say, you simply won't appeal to them – something about the way you blink, speak, or even where you were born. You will lose a certain percentage of people before you enter the room, and that should be expected. Knowing this is important not just in your approach to taking a leadership role, but also in your friendships and your career.

Do you get every job you apply to? Of course not. So you can't expect to persuade 100% of anyone in any context.

Outside of some truly extraordinary occurrences, those people are not going to change their minds. Write them off and focus your efforts on the open-minded and ultimately persuadable. Seek rejection as quickly as possible so you can turn your attention to those with whom you have a better chance and that actually matter.

So what do we do with this realization? We can find pinpoint what exactly we should be looking for - how can you deduce if someone is open to what you have to say, or if you are wasting your time attempting to lead and persuade them?

How Can You Tell If Someone Is Persuadable?

The following can tell you if you are going to be wasting your time with your persuasion efforts:

- Do they have the ability or even the means to do what is suggested? *Capable?*
- Does it further an ultimate goal of theirs?
- Is it characteristic of them?
- Are they open-minded?
- Have they supported stances like yours in the past?
- Are they focused only on the present, or can they focus on longer-term goals?
- How objective can they be?
- Are they driven by reason or emotion?
- What do they have to *gain* by switching to your side?
- What do they have to *lose* by switching to your side?
- Does it satisfy a secondary goal of theirs?

The good news is that this persuadable population is actually bigger than you think. Many people think that the only individuals who are persuadable are people who have already expressed a positive inclination toward something.

The persuadable portion of any crowd also includes people who do not yet have enough information. These are people who are simply unsure. It is crucial that you accurately identify the pool of people that can be persuaded as quickly as possible.

The next step is to figure out the context and approach that will enable you to persuade the persuadable.

What's In It For Me?

As all salespeople can attest, you need to walk a mile in the other person's shoes. Focus on what they gain, and how you can address certain problems and issues that they have. In other words, focus on what's in it for them.

All people, regardless of background, what they look like, their education level, and experience have two common truths: we are all going to die one day and we are all selfish.

At some level everyone wants to know, "What's in it for me?"

Because you know that everyone all shares this concern, to persuade a persuadable person, you need to attack from that perspective. Too many persuaders have failed because they get caught up in the features of a proposal or solution.

No one cares about this and this is a completely backwards way to persuade.

Your focus should be on why you expect people to follow you instead of actually giving them a reason to. The former approach benefits only you, while the latter approach benefits the people you want to appeal to.

To get what you want, you must first get people what they want. By putting other people first, we actually take care of our own needs. Notice how most of the above questions about who is persuadable directly or indirectly attempt to find out if you are serving their selfish need.

For example, for something as simple as deciding at what restaurant to eat, it's as easy as basic as framing your considerations on the following: how close is the restaurant to someone's home; how much do they crave a particular kind of food; whether they've previously mentioned they wanted to eat there; how cheap it is; how convenient and quick it is, and so on.

Here's the thing about the unpersuadable and unleadable (by you). You will never be able to get them what they want, or they can't envision you providing for them in that way. The strongest attribute of persuasion is missing: helping people be selfish. Another reason to focus only on those you can persuade.

Remember Einstein's definition of insanity: attempting an action many times and expecting a different result.

It is literally insane to keep trying to persuade those who won't accept you. It has nothing to do with you and everything to do with them. If you can objectively prove your worth and force them to recognize it, you might be able to make leeway. But until you can do that, you need to spend your efforts on those who are receptive and those who need more information and create fervent followers out of them! For every person that will hate your persuasive style, there is at least one with whom it will resonate loudly.

Willpower And Persuasion

One final note by way of famous dictators Fidel Castro and Joseph Stalin – every one of us has a certain amount of willpower throughout the day. It's easy to refuse to eat a donut the first time, but if that donut is constantly in front of you, and people keep asking if you want one, eventually you're going to cave.

Castro and Stalin were infamous for scheduling 4:00 AM meetings because they would be exhausted, their willpower would be weak, and they simply wouldn't want to be there. They would agree more easily to whatever was suggested because they just wanted to go back to sleep and try to salvage their night.

They were at a point where they just wanted instant gratification, and that desire vetoed their resistance to what was suggested.

Not everyone may be persuadable by you, but you might be able to catch them (or manufacture) at times where their sense of decision fatigue, general fatigue, and exhaustion can work for you.

Chapter 3. Creating Emotional Debt

One particularly effective technique that will boost your persuasiveness is the law of reciprocity.

There's a barista at my local café who occasionally gives me a free croissant – about once every two weeks. It's a small gesture and testament to how much I patronize the café. I'm sure that she does this because I'm a familiar face that occasionally brightens her day with jokes. She starts making my order as soon as she sees me waiting in line.

I highly doubt she has an ulterior motive –she's just making my day better. So when she asked if I was interested in contributing to a charity she was promoting, it was a no-brainer for me. Why did I respond that way? It was a little bit of an emotional debt, but mostly I wanted to subtly acknowledge that I appreciate what she does for me on a bi-weekly basis.

The law of reciprocity is something that we've all experienced. When someone does something nice for you, any small gesture, you will almost always feel compelled to reciprocate. Often, you don't hesitate even if your gesture is

Doing things for others, no matter how small will cause others to do things for you

far bigger than the original act because that still evens the score between you. It's the positive version of "An eye for an eye" which is a promise of vengeance.

It is human nature to feel indebted to people who perform small acts for you, and it's almost instinctive to say "I got you next time" or something similar. Why do we do this?

Two main reasons. First, it is customary to reply to kindness with kindness. It's how you show the kind of person you are and match up to the generosity and kindness the other person has shown you. It's to keep up with expectations. Second, it's an attempt to avoid appearing ungrateful or, worse, oblivious.

Whatever the case, if you are the person performing small acts for others as a leader can, it's a way you can take advantage of people's emotions to persuasively lead them.

The law of reciprocity is effective because it is so subtle. Often people do not even realize they are engaging in reciprocal behavior. They might not realize they are acting in a way that is beneficial to you just to fulfill some nagging in their head. All they know is they feel compelled to follow your lead.

The best way to keep it subtle and under the radar is to trigger it with small tokens of kindness and acts that endear you to others.

These are the actions that make people assume you are a certain type of person and think, "There goes Patrick again, such a generous guy."

Their hardwired primal psychology tends to exaggerate the goodness you extended to them, and they cannot help but want to repay you. At the very least, they will repay you by looking at you in a completely different and positive light.

If someone helps you with a work project, or brings you coffee when you are busy working, how do you feel about that person? You feel warmth, but also awareness that you want to repay them for their kindness. Payback does not necessarily have to involve exact repayment in kind. Somebody could be kind to you by giving you their time and you can repay them by taking them out to lunch. Reciprocity takes different forms.

You can't go wrong with the law of reciprocity because when you know what you are doing, you can trigger this almost automatic response in people and it does not have to cost you much.

Keep in mind that, unlike the more obvious examples above, reciprocity can take different forms depending on the person. Some people view it in terms of an act of service or gift, but there are other ways of paying back someone acting for you, such as even a simple word, pat on the back, or spending time with someone when they are down.

The law of reciprocity also works on a more direct level than gaining compliance through emotional debt.

Imagine that you've performed a favor for someone – they have benefitted directly from you already. They now view

Create positive associations in all interactions

Hanging out w/ me should result in good things

you as a source of positivity, someone that can possibly continue to benefit them in the future. Remember that people are mostly self-centered. It's like the baby bird that initially loves its mother because she is the primary source of food.

If they act nice to you, they recognize that they can curry more favor with you, which ultimately benefits them even more. They've gotten a taste and they want more.

In a way, you've created a mutually beneficial relationship where the primary motivation is simply to be nice to each other.

Chapter 4. Speak People's Languages (Communication Styles)

It may surprise you, but I had difficulty communicating with my parents when I went through my angsty, angry, teenager phase.

Part of it was attributable to the fact that I was openly rebelling and trying to claim my own identity in the way that only teenagers do, but part of it, in hindsight, was also because the three of us (my parents and me) had vastly different communication styles.

We could all be trying to convey and accomplish exactly the same thing, but the way we communicated would irk one of us and would cause more discord than it should have.

For example, take my father – very analytical and no-nonsense. That didn't resonate well with a teenager who was operating on a personal and emotional level.

Different people have different communication styles. This should not come as a surprise.

We come from different backgrounds and we have different experiences. As a result, we have learned to communicate in different ways that have worked in our different walks of life. This applies to our love languages, learning styles, and everything else we can think of. Some of us like baseball more than football. It happens.

No one's style is better, but being aware of the frameworks that people operate in can help you connect with them better to ultimately persuade them to your way of thinking.

If you aren't aware of the different styles, you might be wasting a lot of effort trying to convert people or talk to them in a way they don't respond well to. If your goal is to convince someone of something, you had better speak their language.

When it comes to communication styles, there are four main types:
- Analytical
- Intuitive
- Personal
- Functional

One major philosophical difference that distinguishes these four styles from each other is the extent to which a person communicates with emotions or with data.

If someone communicates more through data and analysis, they might say something like, "This has been a good year; we have 10% growth in sales." Someone who communicates more through emotion and connection would say, "I'm happy with our performance, I feel like we're having a great year."

Try to find the style that fits you best, and then take a look around at the people you seek to persuade and what style fits them best. You'll find an overlap you should operate within to best make your persuasive points and arguments.

Analytical Communicators

If you're an analytical person, you like hard data and real numbers. You tend to be suspicious or skeptical of people who are not in command of the facts and data. You typically like very specific and carefully selected language.

You dislike vague or "flexible" language. For example, when somebody tells you, "Sales are positive." You get frustrated because you feel that statement doesn't really give you much to work with. You're thinking what exactly does this "positive" mean? Are we up 5.2 percent, or are we up 22 percent? Give me a number.

People with an analytical communication style have little patience for people who communicate with their hearts. They don't like emotional talk. The advantage of having an analytical communication style is that you are able to look at issues logically and dispassionately. You filter information through your head, not your heart. But, according to a research study, most consumers make buying decisions on a purely emotional level. When they are asked to explain their decisions, however, they come up with seemingly logical and analytical explanations.

What is the downside of having an analytical communication style? Well, first of all, people might think you're cold or you don't care. When interacting with people who are emotional, who are warm and chatty, it's easy for you to look like grumpy or unapproachable. It's easy for you to be a killjoy because you tend to ask questions that disrupt their feel-good narrative.

It's also easy for you to get irritated and tensed at people who use very fuzzy language. You have a tendency to look at things in a very dispassionate, emotional, and numbers driven way. This tends to have a very negative effect when you are in a political situation.

For example, if you are in a work group, you might develop a lot of enemies right around promotion time because it may seem to others that you are always shooting people down. This is especially true when you're in a work group and you have somebody who is an emotional influence leader. This person is good at motivating people. However, if you're always peppering them with facts and requiring them to logically explain their position, this makes you look disruptive. This makes you look like a person who has an axe to grind.

The solution: speak to these people, using terms they like and using positions they understand. You don't have to abandon your analytical communication style. You just need to be sensitive to the emotions at play so you can subtly massage in the necessary facts and logic in a way the emotional crowd you're dealing with can hear and absorb them.

Intuitive Communicator

Intuitive communicators are people who look at the big picture. They're not all that worried about tiny details. They don't like getting bogged down by numbers, details, and statistics. Also, they like to cut right to the chase. They don't like to be walked through all the logical progressions and get an idea regarding the different details that fit together to create an outcome. They don't have the patience for that.

Instead, they want to get a feel for what the real issue is. They also need to get a feel for how the things you're talking about fit with a broader overview. For example, some people, like functional communicators, will tell you things using a step by step process. They start with point A and go to point B, then point C, and on to D, E, and so on. If you are an intuitive person, that kind of explanation will bore you to tears. In fact, it will make you want to catapult yourself through the nearest window. You want to say, "Okay, okay, but what is the conclusion? What is the bottom line?"

One big plus of having an intuitive communication style is that your communication is quick and to the point. You're all about business. You're all about seizing an opportunity when it's red hot. You're also very comfortable with big ideas and you are an out-of-the-box thinker. Because you're so good at thinking big, you enjoy challenging conventions. You like breaking myths and long held assumptions.

Intuitive communicators may not always have enough patience when dealing with a situation that requires attention to detail. Because they get impatient, they run the risk of missing an important point. This can lead them to make faulty decisions. Typically, intuitive communicators have the most difficulty dealing with functional communicators. It's like talking Spanish to somebody who speaks Japanese. It's going to be very difficult. Intuitive people find it hard to deal with process driven, methodical, step-by-step and detail oriented people.

The solution: identify the communication style of the person you're speaking with and patiently walk them through the steps while at the same time reminding them of the big picture. Usually when you do this, they will tend to speed up or at least summarize certain parts thus reducing your chances of getting bored.

Functional Communicator

You like process, details, and time lines. You have an eye for detail. You also like to communicate things in a step-by-step fashion. Nothing scares you more than missing a detail. You think that if a particular element is missing, it will lead to your making the wrong decision. You're very fearful of that happening.

If you're a functional thinker, the big advantage is you hit the necessary details. Usually, decisions that are fully informed have a higher likelihood of being the right decisions. Since you step through the details in a very granular way, all the details are there and nothing is missed. When you're in a group, work, or political setting, people often turn to you to be the person implementing the program. Why? They have a tremendous amount of confidence in your love for process and detail. They know you will not cut corners or take shortcuts.

Another advantage of being a functional communicator is that you can contribute to your group tremendously by playing the devil's advocate. You know all the details. Accordingly, you know all the potential weak spots. You can then throw out scenarios to pick everybody's brain so you can build on your strengths and improve on whatever shortcomings the project has.

The big downside here is appearing boring and slow. You see, most people don't have the luxury of time. In this day and age of the internet and lightning fast communications, people have a functional version of ADHD. We like our facts in short bite-sized pieces. We don't like to chew on our facts. As much as possible, we like decisions that are prepackaged – for better or for worse.

When you come across people and you talk in a functional way and you get caught up in detail, you end up losing the attention of your audience. This is especially true if you're dealing with "big picture" or intuitive communicators. They don't like details. They want to see the introduction and then they want you to skip all the way to the end, to the conclusion. They could care less about the details.

So, how do you function in this situation?

Well, since you know the details, and you know the broad picture, you might want to give enough information to properly cement the introduction and just enough details to properly support the conclusion and leave it at that. No extras. I know, this is very difficult to do at first because you'd rather dive into the nitty gritty. You'd rather get into the guts of the internal processes, statistics, data, and numbers involved. But you need to resist that temptation. Instead, give enough information to support the introduction, get to the point of why people should care, and then talk about the conclusion and only the top three factors that support that conclusion. Keep it short and sweet and try to be interesting.

Personal Communicator

If you're a personal communicator, you value emotional language. When you communicate with people, you really savor the human to human connection and this is what drives you. You use the personal connection as your mode of discovering what others are really thinking. You find value in assessing, not just how people think but how they feel. You tend to be a good listener and a diplomat. You can smooth over conflicts and you're typically concerned with the health of your numerous relationships. You really care about people, you love stepping into other people's shoes and feeling what they're feeling.

The big advantage of personal communicators is they tend to develop really deep personal relationships. You are able to achieve a tremendous amount of personal intimacy with the people you communicate with. After talking with you, people walk away with the impression that you truly "get them." You are the glue that holds your social circle together. People run to you for advice. Talking to you makes others feel motivated. You are like the spiritual center of your group of friends or family members.

The big disadvantage of this type of communication is it's too easy for you to take things personally. It's also too easy for you to think with your heart instead of with your brain. There may be certain logical processes you are all too eager to overlook, discount, or assume and this can lead to catastrophic decisions. This is especially true when dealing with people with a track record.

You tend to give people the benefit of the doubt in situations where someone who tends to be more logical would say, "Well, this person has a track record of failure, why are you going to give this person another chance?" And not surprisingly, personal communicators often end up feeling betrayed. You often read rosy emotional judgments into situations that don't deserve such a reading.

If you're a personal communicator and you're dealing with somebody who's analytical, you might want to step away from your feelings and focus more on the numbers that person is talking about and try to accept the logical connections between information shared by that person. Of course, you can always tie this into the human dimension or the human consequence of an otherwise cold and logical decision, but you might want to minimize that. Otherwise, the analytical speaker might feel you are making decisions based solely on your emotions instead of on statistics, data, and logic (which make more sense to them).

Can you identify what your style is, and the style of the people you interact with the most?

Speak someone's communication style to make your point

and appeal to what matters the most to them. Otherwise, you're just speaking another language and your persuasion is already fighting an uphill battle.

Chapter 5. Likability As Lubricant

A couple of careers ago, I was a personal trainer.

Technically, I was above average. I knew more than most trainers I knew, and could put together workouts that would leave you curled up in fetal position...in a good way. However, plenty of trainers knew more than I did but were not as successful.

A personal trainer's entire job is to motivate and lead someone through something that they know will be incredibly unpleasant. It's not the same as in a work context where, for example, you might not want to fill out another spreadsheet – it's a physical challenge that can literally leave you unable to walk the next day.

But my clients never had any motivation problems because they *liked me*. I could relate with them, and my primary goal was to make them laugh through their entire workout. They would do sets and reps, and the workout portion seemed like interruptions in funny conversations between us.

That's what I mean when I say that likability is persuasion's lubricant. People will do things for and follow people they like and are charmed by. If you can make them forget about the task at hand, or create an additional motivation of wanting to comply with you, your challenge in persuading them is already half done.

Now you have the unenviable task of trying to evaluate yourself on an objective basis – *are you likable,* whether in social or work settings?

If you're a manager or supervisor, there is typically an unspoken yet tangible divide in relationships between managers and subordinates (or simply those seeking to lead, and those following). You can be as likable as possible, but you likely won't be connecting on the same level as a peer because of the inherent power imbalance.

For the same reason that it's often difficult, or flat-out unusual, to be friends with your teacher or professor, an imbalanced relationship doesn't function like a normal friendship. Co-workers inevitably complain about their boss and their workload, sometimes as a matter of reflex, which obviously isn't possible if the person who has created that workload is present.

Given that you can't (and many times shouldn't) connect and be likable on the normal friend level, your likability as a leader will be based on your trustworthiness, on your ability to make sure people feel heard, and your making them feel valuable as equals.

That's a point worth repeating again to drive it home.

You won't be able to connect with most people if you are not inherently at the same level as they are – you simply don't have the same problems and concerns. Therefore, you have to focus on being likable from a subordinate's perspective, and that requires trust, validation, and respect.

The truth is being likable and being charming in any social or work context is learned behavior. And just as likable and charming people have learned to be that way, you can too.

How can you communicate respect, trust, and validation?

It's the little things.

If you think about it, most people either don't have the luxury or simply are too lazy to get to know each other on a deep and profound level. They are always looking for shortcuts and shorthand signals that will speed up the process.

You need to be aware of this reality so you can focus on sending the shortcuts that allow people to read respect, trust, and validation.

Respect
- Always ask, never tell.
- Tell people they are valuable.
- Respectfully and graciously disagree.
- Always apologize when it is due.

Trust
- Tell people you know they can handle it.
- Keep true to your word.

- Be reliable.
- Use objective fairness; no favorites.

Validation
- Give credit early and often.
- Never dismiss people outright.
- Notice and praise people's efforts.
- Celebrate small victories.

As long as you know how people operate mentally, you can trigger the emotions you seek.

When people like you as a leader in whatever context that's when the floodgates open. People will feel a sense of obligation and duty to you that they would never feel if they didn't feel connected to you.

They won't want to let you down! When you can cause people to react with their own emotions, you don't have to do much outward persuading yourself. This is the zone where people start to say "I'd follow them to hell and back!"

All aspects of your life stand to gain if you pay serious attention to what likability means in different contexts. And once you create likability, you can get where you want to be.

A final aspect of likability is how similar you may appear to the person you are trying to lead or persuade. Unlike the contextual definition of liking described earlier, this kind of likability is universal.

It's arguably hardwired into our primal brains. Thousands of years ago, if our ancestors didn't discriminate when deciding who to like and trust, chances are strong that we wouldn't be here today. Trust someone from a different tribe and you might end up with a spear in your back – it's a self-preservation mechanism that we are drawn to similarity.

It's also just easier to connect with someone when you're more alike. You have more to talk about, you think alike, and you share a similar set of values. You're also more eager to connect with them and actually be friends. It's pretty compelling when you meet someone from your high school, or your childhood neighborhood, isn't it? You assume that they are on your level, and that's an underrated aspect of connection.

You can exploit this hardwired tendency. First, subtly fish for details about people's lives and show an interest in their interests. It's not something you haven't heard before, but presenting your interest in *their* interest as a similarity (and not just curiosity) is the key. Of course, through this process it's common that you'll discover actual shared interests, as well as "small world" moments – you both did X and Y, where X and Y are relatively rare actions. If you can tap into a "small world" moment early, then your likability will shoot through the roof.

Second, you can appear more similar on a superficial level. Everyone has a different vibe that they send out, whether they realize it or not. This shows in their speech, body language, gesticulation, energy level, vocal tonality, speech rate, and the amount of eye contact they engage in when speaking. In other words, the more you can mirror someone's general demeanor, the more comfortable they will feel with you and ultimately like you. Your perspectives are so similar that they feel they understand you. You are relatable.

Regardless, likability makes persuasion easy because you don't have to persuade. People tend to drop their guard around people they like, and even more so around people that they want to like them.

Likability takes people's basic question, "What's in it for me" and turns it into "What's in it for us," where you are part of the "us."

Chapter 6. Manufacturing External Credibility

Sometimes we blindly follow others, and it's usually reasonable in context because of their credibility.

The last time I blindly followed someone I was a teenager trying to improve my soccer skills. My parents had somehow obtained the contact information of a former national team player who lived around our neighborhood. He had some free time and was willing to tutor me a couple of hours a week.

Obviously, this was amazing, and I told myself that no matter how insane his methods might be, I would obey them exactly because in all likelihood they would produce amazing results.

Some of his drills and exercises made instant sense to me, and I could see how they directly correlated to an increase in my ball-handling or agility. Other days led me to wonder if he was trying to "Miyagi" me (as in *The Karate Kid*) with endless repetition of seemingly unrelated and pointless activities that would somehow translate into soccer skills.

They did not.

For a number of other reasons, I stopped working with him after about a month, but I'll never forget him because of how blindly I followed him. It was because he was so credible – one of the best players in the country shouldn't be questioned, right?

Even though I didn't find him particularly trustworthy, or nice for that matter, it didn't matter because he had massive external validation that, in my mind, made him beyond reproach.

Credibility is powerfully persuasive, and sometimes we assign it more value than it deserves. But that can work for you.

Credibility is mostly proven in two ways.

First, you can prove your credibility through pure demonstration of skill and knowledge until people realize that you know what you are talking about. After all, seeing is believing. You show them what you are capable of. If you can run through the gauntlet and prove yourself worthy, then you deserve to be labeled an authority with a leadership role.

This is our preferred way of learning because we are able to examine all the evidence in front of our face and see through those who can only talk the talk. Can they perform or not? Unfortunately, this is precisely the type of time-intensive process that is quite rare in our world, as most of us don't have the luxury of that kind of time.

In other words, it's tough to prove your credibility simply by showing it because no one has the patience for this process.

That's where external validation, as with the national team soccer player, comes in. In most cases, people are validated externally by reputation, hearsay, or word of mouth.

This means that people will determine your credibility and authority level based not on what you do or demonstrate, but on your reputation and what other people say about you – before you even say a word. If enough people say that you are an expert on something, eventually people will consider you an authority in that particular subject, and any failures will be attributed to momentary lapses instead of a lack of expertise.

We're at the mercy of other people's assessment of you!

Just as the right referral can open a lot of doors when you are looking for a job, the right referral can make you an instant authority. Who do you need to refer you so rank and file members of the particular audience you are trying to reach will find you credible?

To become an authority in any area, you have to have existing authorities vouch for you. You are borrowing their authority and taking it as your own.

This should be your road map when it comes to persuading. It is too tempting to jump into any kind of situation and try to take the bull by the horns to try to impress everybody with what you know.

Instead of wasting so much time trying to prove yourself directly to others, get referred and introduced. Refer to relevant data points that make you worth following. If you are trying to make a grand entrance into any kind of social circle, make sure that you lay the groundwork first.

From a purely efficiency perspective, this makes the most sense. When you try to impress a group of people, you are going to have to repeat the same shtick many times in front of many groups of people. To become credible by getting referred by an existing authority, you only need to impress one person at a time.

Always try to get yourself introduced to new contacts by someone who has a level of authority, even if you don't know them that well. They carry weight. Don't be afraid to invoke someone's name or get their recommendation for small things.

Merely being on some people's radar can be extremely valuable. Be strategic about who you get to know based on their reach. Seek small ways that you get people's stamp of approval and signoff, even if it's just a rubber stamp.

Just don't make it seem as if you are relying on them – use their credibility to bolster your own skills and credentials.

Beyond others' words about you, you will also gain a degree of external validation if you have certain authority indicators such as training, pedigree, and degrees. If you go to the right school, if you have the right degrees, or you have a certain accreditation, people will automatically grant you a certain level of authority. It's like a reflex.

This is just a variation of the expert validation I described earlier, but you are relying on people's ingrained respect of institutions rather than their reliance on the opinions of others. There's a reason that listing your accomplishments and pedigree will get you a return phone call far quicker than anything else.

People just do not have the luxury of time to wait for you to demonstrate that you know what you know. Instead, as a shortcut, they willingly rely on a respected third party's referral or a recognized institution's accreditation of your expert or authority status.

But there are two problems with these objective indicators of credibility. People often gain respect solely because they possess them and for no other reason and they are simply not attainable by everyone. So they are not a solution to the credibility problem, they are simply "nice to haves."

So what if you don't have these external sources of credibility? What can you substitute to get external credibility?

Social proof: "Everyone I've mentioned this to you has jumped at the opportunity."

Positive results: "It's the absolute best way."

Extreme confidence: "I'm 100% positive this is the way to go."

It's all about perception.

The key lesson underlying persuasion is that there are ways to make actual persuasion unnecessary – and that's the perception of personal power. People won't take you seriously if they don't feel that the words coming out of your mouth and your actions carry any weight.

That's what credibility does, just as it did with that soccer player. It made him virtually unquestionable, and one might argue that I had to be persuaded away from listening to him. That kind of external validation is one of the most powerful currencies, and there are multiple ways you can create mental links to it.

Chapter 7. Elements of Persuasive Presentation

Most of us think that we know how to present topics, arguments, and statistics to be persuasive. But do we?

Some elements of what creates an overall persuasive presentation might be intuitive and second nature for you to appeal to. We might even do these things unconsciously.

For example, we become passionate and excited about what we try to convey. We try to poke holes in the other person's arguments while trying to appear unbiased. We intuitively highlight our own benefits while downplaying or outright omitting our Achilles heels.

The goal of this book is not to just skim things that you already know. The goal is to go deeper and discover what you didn't know that makes people think twice – or *not* think and simply act in your favor.

Just to cover all the bases, let's go through some of the factors that you may already know and employ first to persuade people with your presentation.

Even if you think you know them, it's still helpful to articulate exactly what is happening in each of them so you can replicate them in any situation. Much of the criteria in this chapter for what makes someone persuasive come from psychological studies by Zakary Rucker and Derek Tormala, psychologists who specialize in studying persuasion and social influence.

Accuracy

We are more easily persuaded when we perceive the information we receive to be accurate, not doctored, and not spun or editorialized in any way. This is why arguments that pertain to real data, objective statements, and replicable results are so convincing – and also why presenting anecdotes as evidence are persuasively weak.

We want to ensure that we are basing our decisions on accurate information.

If it's inaccurate, we have the benefit of putting the responsibility and accountability on someone else, but that still leaves us in a bad spot where we've made a bad decision.

"You got the figures wrong? Well, that's why I bought this phone! I can't believe you would do that!"

To imply accuracy, you make references to how you know something is verified, and frequently refer to third-party sources that have their own source of legitimacy. You are borrowing the authority of others to make your presentation appear more accurate and legitimate.

Relevance

We are more easily persuaded when the information presented is more directly relevant to our own situation or context.

This means that the closer to our experience an example is, the more we believe in its truth and that it will have similar effects on us. In other words, whatever is being sought will transfer seamlessly to your situation.

For example, if you are a soccer player looking for new soccer cleats, which of the following arguments would be more persuasive?

"I'm not a soccer player, I'm more of a karate guy, but these soccer cleats seem pretty popular,"

or:

"I used to play soccer professionally, and I would recommend these soccer cleats for grass and turf alike."

The difference is that the former argument showed a lack of relevance to your situation. The salesperson didn't play soccer, so how could they possibly know the standards and whether their words were true? The latter argument is highly relevant because the salesperson knows what they are talking about, and thus you believe that the benefits will transfer to your situation.

You want to present a situation with as many elements as possible that people can relate to in their own life and situation.

Perceived Importance of Information

We are more easily persuaded when we believe that a piece of information is a central element of the overall argument, versus an ancillary matter.

This is more easily seen through illustration.

For example, if you want to persuade someone to purchase a television, a more effective persuasive argument would be to talk about how important that particular television size is for their preferences rather than the color of the remote control. The first argument is an important metric of the television set, while the other isn't something that will move the needle for 99.99% of people.

This aspect of persuasive presentation is to focus on the most important and central aspects of your overall argument to make whatever you are saying appear significant and important.

Of course, it's a separate persuasion technique to make whatever you are talking about *appear* to be one of the important aspects of the television so as to inflate the value of what you are saying.

However, if you have to resort to this, you may not be able to shake the impression that you are grasping at straws and don't have an actual relevant argument to make. Following the above example, this would be when you attempt to make the remote control appear to be the most important aspect of buying a television because it's what you will be physically touching the most. Not too convincing, but that's what happens when you don't have a solid argument otherwise.

Affective Validation

Rucker and Tormala essentially describe this element of persuasive presentation as a subjective feeling when a decision simply *feels right*.

Obviously, this is impossible to quantify. How can we make sure that something just *feels right* for someone to say "yes" to?

We can't do that with the topic or argument inherently. Since affective validation is subjective, that means it is based on the emotions we experience with other people. Therefore, if you can work hard to make yourself perceived as trustworthy, likable, vulnerable, and looking out for the other person's best interests, more often than not, *you* will simply feel right to those you are attempting to convince.

If you build enough comfort and trust, what persuades other people won't be your actual arguments – it will be *you*. It will be how they feel about you, and whether they feel like they are willing to take a leap of faith based on that assessment.

Affective validation is the difference between coming off like a used car salesman with slicked back hair who calls you "their kind of people," and someone about whom you would say "I liked their vibe."

Other People

It has been well-documented that using phrases such as "Experts agree" is an extremely effective marketing tactic.

This draws upon the phenomenon of *social proof and consensus*. Simply put, if you are made aware that other people have agreed to a certain argument or proposal, you are more likely to go along with it because you feel comfortable coasting on the decision struggles of other people.

You assume that everyone else has wrestled with the same dilemma as you, and since they have all come to a consensus, that is the correct decision for you as well. It can be as basic as saying, "Everyone else in this neighborhood went along with it, what about you?"

You also assume that any negatives or shortcomings will have been considered by other people, and deemed inconsequential in making the decision. In other words, everyone else did it and didn't find a problem with it, so it must be a safe or correct decision.

Maybe we shouldn't make these assumptions, but we as humans look for shortcuts as often as possible, and someone else saying "I was just like you, and I chose this" is one of the best and most helpful shortcuts possible.

Of course, there are problems with the psychology of social

proof and consensus. We find safety in numbers, which means that careful consideration of the merits isn't usually a deciding factor. When you invoke the fact that other people, similar or identical in position or context, have made a similar decision, you make it easy for people to say "yes" to you.

Ease

This is the first of three persuasion tactics that are much less obvious, yet still deadly effective.

In fact, it's so subtle that researchers were taken by surprise when they confirmed their findings. A 2007 study by Rucker and Tormala took a group of university students and divided them into two groups. The first group was given an assignment to list two arguments for a policy, which was considered the easy group in terms of the task. The second group was to list ten arguments for the same policy, which was deemed the difficult group in terms of the task.

The first group, the group that had the objectively easier task of listing only two arguments, displayed significantly greater confidence and persuasion in their arguments for the policy. They supported the policy more, and were more persuaded to the policy in general.

Another study by Norwick and Epley came to the same conclusion. The researchers showed subjects simple questionnaires with fonts and colors that were either tough or easy to read, but identical in content. The group of subjects that had the questionnaires that were easy to read felt more confident in their responses.

Both groups of researchers found that if there are subjective feelings of ease associated with a concept, people simply like them more and they are easy to persuade people over to. Ease, simplicity, and reduction are great contributors to persuasive presentation.

This explains why simple, short marketing slogans can be so powerful. We prefer things to be simple, even though they often are not. When we see something that appears to be simple, we want to trust it at face value. This is another piece of evidence that shows persuasion to be affected more emotionally than logically.

This is a simple persuasive tactic.

Make your arguments, proposals, and stances as easy to digest and understand as possible, even if that means they aren't 100% accurate in scope. After all, you *should* be able to summarize your stances or arguments in one sentence – otherwise they aren't good to begin with. Whenever there is a possibility of complications, err on the side of generalizing and oversimplifying. Think in terms of slogans, mottos, and easy to remember phrases. If ever in doubt, simplify everything possible, from the font to the language used. Statistics generally put non-verbal communication at somewhere between 55% - 93% of the message that is understood, and it is no different with persuasion.

People don't like to spend a lot of time thinking, so help them not have to.

Defense

Become a devil's advocate.

Studies by Rucker and Petty showed that when people defended a position, proposal, or stance from verbal attacks, they became more solidified in that position.

Essentially, when you verbalize and articulate justifications for a position, you begin to believe them yourself, even if that wasn't your initial stance. It's as if saying these things out loud makes you agree with them more and see the logic behind them.

What does that mean for you?

It means that if you are trying to convince someone to do something, decry the act and ask them for reasons why they should and how they will benefit. They may argue for the act and persuade themselves that it is a good idea.

If you want someone's belief to grow stronger in something, ask them why they think that, and what they would say to critics of it. Let them articulate their thoughts out loud and grow more impassioned as they hear themselves.

If you want someone to *not* do something, ask them why they shouldn't, and what they think the possible consequences of not doing it will be. Encourage them to be reminded of everything they feel in an organized, convincing fashion.

You are just posing questions to them that make them say

their reasons out loud and argue against you, thus confirming and reinforcing their beliefs.

Completeness

Completeness is the final aspect of persuasive presentation.

What exactly does this mean? People are somewhat cognizant and aware that you are biased. Everyone is, in one way or another. You might even be outwardly biased, in which case, people are even more aware of the fact that they have to take whatever you say with a grain of salt. Simply put, they might not trust you because of where your interests lay. You might be trying to persuade them of something that is completely against their self-interest.

If you want people to choose a restaurant because it's "amazing" but also within walking distance for you, then people have good reason to doubt you, especially if it's a thirty minute drive for them.

The way to get around this perception of possible bias is to be complete. Present a complete argument, including pros and cons of your proposal, stance, or opinion. Even if you don't represent them completely faithfully and accurately, you are still avoiding the label of being biased because you have addressed everything to present a complete view.

It's even more powerful if you can be the first to address the top two arguments against your proposal. You can choose how to frame the arguments, and how to successfully defuse them. Be the one to bring them up so you aren't on the defensive with them.

For example, if you want to persuade someone to buy a motorcycle, you can't just talk about the benefits of easy parking, quick transport, and great gas mileage. You have to be the first to address the top concerns of safety and theft, and then control the argument and analysis such that the pros outweigh the cons.

Presentation can make or break your persuasive overtures. Carefully review this chapter and make sure that you are hitting the mark on these tactics, otherwise you run the risk of immediately being seen as transparent and invalidated.

Chapter 8. Exact Persuasive Phrases

The previous chapter focused on persuasive presentation – that is, the underlying components of persuasive statements and arguments.

In a way, it's similar to marketing. If you're in marketing, or familiar with it, you may have recognized the elements that you need for a successful marketing campaign, such as the reasons marketers like to use celebrity endorsements, or what makes an advertisement go viral versus languishing in obscurity.

There are even more specific ways to speak and use phrasing to persuade, win people over, and generally get them to do what you want.

When I was in college, I had a psychology professor who, if you only listened to him speak, was the most accomplished psychologist since Freud. I wasn't quite sure how he did it, but with each lecture, my impression of him as a giant in the field grew exponentially.

Naturally, I grew curious about his actual accomplishments,

so after the lecture one day I went home to do some research on him and marvel in awe. What I found was somewhat startling. He had a few publications, as any professor would, but his standing was not nearly what he touted it to be. He was an adjunct professor, without tenure, and his biggest claim to fame was being a footnote in a much more famous professor's textbook, which he inflated into a long-lasting partnership.

There was a shameless way that he spoke and phrased things that make him seem above doubt and far more accomplished than he really was.

We'll cover some of the tactics he used (consciously or subconsciously, I'll never know), and other ways to make your phrasing as persuasive as possible.

Use Absolutes

It never failed. Whatever he tried, or was involved with, was the best option available, had the best people, and allowed him to be the best.

My professor, and other great persuaders, didn't deal in subtleties or gray areas. Everything that they engaged in, produced, or even did was bar none the best, top of class, or world leading. They had the shamelessness or simple self-promotion gene that allowed them to never leave any doubt that they were great. In other words, they tooted their own horns the most, where most of us would have problems with that out of self-consciousness and fear of appearing arrogant.

If you want to persuade someone to do something, that means everything associated with it, every feature, every benefit, and every review is the best.

If everything about them is the hyperbolic best, that means everything opposing them is the hyperbolic worst. Those are disasters, the worst, tragedies, crippling blows, barely functioning, and unbelievably terrible. If you can possess the shamelessness required for this persuasive phrasing tactic, then you should have no problems not pulling your punches here.

This is your chance to demonstrate how gargantuan the divide is between what you propose and what might keep someone back. Instead of a debate about the features and benefits, you control the conversation and turn it into a black and white option with only one real choice that any sane person would choose.

You might have a hard time digesting this tactic, but accuracy isn't the point here. You're creating an emotional response that will make people react. People subconsciously know that you probably aren't *the best* and others probably aren't *the worst*, but if you keep repeating that hyperbole, there just might be some truth behind it.

Allude to Others

Another huge aspect of persuasive phrasing is to make appeals to other people, whether they are authority figures or not.

The idea is that since other people have been persuaded by

you, or agree with you, that your idea or stance is a sound one. It's a decision by committee!

If possible and applicable, using authority figures in any way possible helps. The way you use them doesn't even have to be directly supporting you and your position, you can merely mention that an authority figure was involved in something, spoke about it, or is affiliated with it. That way, you are borrowing their authority and legitimacy.

If you are unable to evoke authority figures and drop names, then you can allude to others in a very general and fuzzy sense. You can see what I mean below, where key phrases include:

- Many people
- Everyone, everybody
- Lots of people
- Anyone that matters
- Everyone that has common sense
- All the top experts say
- Many studies have shown
- Using "we" instead of "I"

There may not be anyone saying what you are purporting them to say, but that doesn't matter. All that matters is that you are using persuasive phrasing to make people believe that you have massive social proof and support.

Is it lying? Not necessarily. After all, it could technically be true.

"Many people" may indeed make the same persuasive

argument as you have. A couple of "top experts" might also agree, and one "study" has been shown to support your argument. That's just semantics that don't matter when you're trying to persuade someone.

Getting into the habit of alluding to others is something that can make it sound like you have a frenzied mob behind you.

Control the Frame

What does this mean?

First, you need to define your persuasive frame. Your frame is to be one of superior knowledge. If you are trying to persuade someone of something, you are utterly convinced of its genius, and you are coming from a place of experience and knowledge. There is no discussion, because what you say is fact, and what others are say is unresearched, unvalidated, and has multiple holes for you to poke your stick into.

They just don't understand the nuance and subtleties!

Basically, you are creating a persona/character/role where you are right by way of superior knowledge. You are not persuading, so much as educating others on the choices in front of them, which of course, can only lead to the one that you prefer.

The most important point is this: when you control the frame, you control the reality.

This is especially so in the face of doubt or criticism. You are leading them away from the plains and toward the water because you know more than they do. You will express disbelief, disgust, and annoyance that an attack not even worthy of your attention has come to face you.

Reject the criticism, pay it no attention, and act as if they are crazy to bring it up. For example, how would you react if someone tried to argue that dogs were as smart as humans on account of a study they read from the National Enquirer? That's the exact tone and mood of setting and controlling the frame here.

The pitfalls of this approach are pretty obvious. You can easily come across as a condescending and arrogant jerk. However, if you use the right tone and delivery, you can pull it off as someone who wants the best for others. Change their reality.

Absolute Silence

A funny thing happens when you give people silence on purpose. You've created tension, and tension is often something that people try to avoid.

Thus, if you give someone silence, they will speak to fill it. You can make this work for your persuasive purposes by introducing absolute silence after they answer you.

For example:

You: "I think this is the best offer we can do for your salary."

Them: "But I thought my resume would qualify me for a

higher position regardless?"

You: [silence plus eye contact]

Can you imagine how that would make someone feel? An intentional absolute silence is essentially an indirect way of saying "Oh, really now?" in a skeptical and doubtful tone.

When you introduce a silence in response to someone's argument or stance, they want to resolve the tension by filling the silence. When they do that, they almost always begin by trying to explain and justify their last argument. They will give you additional information and essentially begin negotiating with themselves because you've just doubted them subtly.

Let's continue the conversation from above.

You: "I think this is the best offer we can do for your salary."

Them: "But I thought my resume would qualify me for a higher position regardless?"

You: [silence plus eye contact]

Them: "Well... It might make sense for me to start lower, that's true. And I know that I'm much less experienced than others in that position..."

When you give people silence, they want to fill it. You'll get more information than you ever would have, even if you were to ask them directly. If you asked them directly, they might have a rehearsed way of framing something to their favor. When you give them silence, however, you make them react emotionally to avoid discomfort, and that's something that most people don't rehearse for.

"Ultimate Terms"

In his 1953 book, *Ethics of Rhetoric*, Richard Weaver coined what he termed "God terms" and "Devil terms."

The latter are all phrases you want to embrace, and that are essentially concepts you want to be associated with. Accordingly, the latter are all phrases that you want to avoid and characterize your opposition as. Essentially, God terms are common values that you should want to embody and be descriptive of, while devil terms are fatalistic.

To be more persuasive, you should become adept at sprinkling both God and devil terms throughout your oration and rhetoric to create an unconscious, emotional reaction and deviation away from evil and toward the forces of good, so to speak. However, if you overuse God terms, they can subtly turn into devil terms, because people will see that you are being too transparent and manipulative.

God term examples: powerful, guaranteed, free, healthy, exclusive, rare, improved, leading, new, honest, easy, and moral.

Devil term examples: dangerous, uncertain, complex, rejected, fear, hopeless, as-is, common, secondary, risky.

Did you notice how the terms of both categories mirror

each other and are often exact opposites? It's also notable that the terms hit on very primal desires and fears.

It's easy to see how you can persuade someone if you constantly repeat how dangerous, complex, and uncertain their other option is, while your option is guaranteed, rare, and honest. See how directly that frames your persuasive arguments?

Chapter 9. The Classic Challenge

Up to this point in the book, I've talked about persuasion very straightforwardly. I've talked about how to make people follow you by directly appealing to their sense of duty, reciprocation, and commitment. These are clear actions that will result in you becoming a leader.

This chapter presents something a bit different. I'm going to talk about appealing to others' sense of ego and pride, two aspects of human beings that often cause deep, visceral reactions but that most people aren't always aware of. This approach is indirect and flies under the radar unlike likability or building your credibility.

It's otherwise known as reverse psychology. You may have hear the term before, but here's how and exactly why it works.

When I was young, I was essentially coerced into concert pianist training. My piano teacher was a very old, very strict Russian woman who had no qualms about making cutting remarks to a nine-year old.

She was full of fun techniques like smacking my hands with a ruler to ensure they remained straight, or having me play endless scales while she went outside to garden for a bit. She was an ultimate taskmaster because that's how she learned and practiced throughout her pianist career back in Russia.

But undoubtedly, her most effective technique in motivating me was essentially issuing a challenge to my pride. She did this in multiple ways, but it was usually by shaking her head and quietly proclaiming that I should just quit and would never reach the levels she had projected for my potential.

One moment I was transcendent, and the next I was shameful.

The big moment came when there was a sizable competition coming up in two months. She repeatedly muttered about how I wouldn't be ready for it. Guess who became enraged and practiced nonstop for two months to prove her wrong?

Of course, such a direct challenge only worked because I was stubborn and had a lot of pride. I know for a fact that it was her Iron Curtain sensibilities that led her to filter her students this way, and that not all her students were motivated in the same harsh way.

But the direct challenge and *classic reverse psychology* worked wonders for me.

Reverse psychology is when you convey a message or feeling to someone, and the desired end result is actually the opposite of what you are saying.

For example, my piano teacher told me to quit, but in reality she wanted me to work harder.

Or, for example, when you tell someone that you bet they can't get somewhere on time, the usual result is their arriving five minutes before even you do!

It doesn't always have to be so obvious, but when you imply that someone is lacking an ability or capacity of some sort, people will almost always take it upon themselves to prove you wrong.

People don't like being told who they are and what they can't do, nor do they like being labeled and put into a box. Deep down, we all believe that we are three-dimensional characters with deep reserves of skill and ability. We prefer our self-image to be preserved because when it's challenged, it's supremely uncomfortable to come face to face with a reality that doesn't jive with our self-perception.

An emotional response is triggered to protect our ego and self-image. When you issue a challenge to someone, they respond to prove their abilities not only to you, but to themselves.

Never underestimate the power of a person's pride. Whenever the ego is involved or at stake, it becomes easier to influence behavior because you automatically know what motivates a person, or pushes their buttons. You can even argue that it's easier to change deeply entrenched behaviors whenever the ego is involved.

A psychological theory called the reactance theory actually supports the logic of reverse psychology, which is a catch-all layman's term.

A 1976 study put two signs next to each other on a bathroom wall. One sign forbade people from writing on the sign, while the other sign had no mention of writing. Guess which sign was covered edge to edge in graffiti by week's end? The first one.

Reactance theory states that when your freedom is threatened, you feel motivated to perform the prohibited action to prove that your freedom has not been compromised.

Challenging someone to do something indicates that you think someone is a certain type of person, and it gives them the opportunity to redefine your perception of them.

For example, the person who is chronically late may know deep down that he has a problem with tardiness, but how do you think that person defines himself? They do not define themselves as flakes or flawed people who just do not have what it takes to show up on time.

Instead, they define themselves as otherwise great people who now and then just have a tough time showing when they're supposed to. In other words, they define themselves in such a way that it does not impact their ego negatively.

Deep down they can gain some feeling of self-satisfaction because whatever issues they may have are not that bad.

When you tell people that you expect them to perform a certain way, which might be different from how they view themselves, you negatively impact their sense of control and freedom. Reactance theory kicks in – they feel that their sense of control over who they are, and their right to define themselves, is being taken away. Basically, we like to hold onto what our parents (hopefully) instilled in us our about special talents and uniqueness.

This is why reverse psychology is very powerful as a persuasive tool. You can subtly get people to want to do something that they would normally not be inclined to do and they might not even realize why.

Here's another example: a true salesperson might say to a customer, "Are you sure you can afford that? It's a very expensive item and I know many of our customers have lower budgets…."

A comment like this is going to inspire a Pretty Woman moment in most people. If phrased properly and in the right context, it is going to trigger the customer to buy!

With one sentence, the salesperson took away the customer's cherished and treasured right to define himself.

That's the key to using reverse psychology for persuasion. If you know how someone defines themselves, and what they pride themselves on, then you should challenge that in a subtle way.

This is how you galvanize people into action without having to ask directly or coerce them.

If, in work settings, you want to persuade someone to a particular action, you can challenge their sense of punctuality, attention to detail, work quality, judgment, sense of duty, timeliness, creativity, technical skills, people management skills, and so on.

If, in social settings, you want to lead someone to a particular action, you can challenge their sense of humor, wit, taste, character, and so on.

Just remember, it has to be something that they pride themselves on in order for the backdoor challenge to work.

Combine these factors of a subtle delivery and the right context, and you can bet that reverse psychology will work wonders for your persuasion quotient.

Chapter 10. Constructing a Persuasive Frame

There's a great Italian movie called *Life is Beautiful* that in many circles has achieved status similar to that of *The Princess Bride*. If you aren't familiar with either of these movies, just know that they have affected generations of romantic relationships.

There's a scene in *Life is Beautiful* where the main character is working as a waiter in a restaurant whose kitchen has already closed, but a man walks in expecting to be served a late dinner.

The main character knows that there is only one choice of entrée and appetizer available, so he uses persuasive situational framing to achieve his goal.

He talks about how delicious and juicy the existing entrée and appetizer are, and when he describes other choices (which are actually non-existent), he describes tastes and textures that couldn't possibly appeal to anyone.

One choice is award-winning, while the other is barely

adequate. One is juicy and luscious, while the other reminds one of sand and is for those who love the taste of pure salt. One will make you full, while the other is a portion that children seem to enjoy. One is healthy, the other is for those on their "cheat days."

Of course, the diner chooses the option that has been framed in glowing terms, which in actuality is the only existing option.

When you present one choice as gold (Option A) and the other as lead (Option B), it's no contest which will be chosen.

How do you do this? By emphasizing the benefits of Option A and emphasizing the negatives of Option B. And most importantly, you do not bend the truth. You just state the truth with repetition and occasional omission.

I say "occasional omission" because if you dismiss the negatives of Option B altogether, you lose credibility and appear uninformed. You just want to maximize the impact of the positives within the big picture of Option A. Proper framing is really about stacking information a certain way.

Here's a list of actions so you can see how this works visually:

Option A (your choice)
- Emphasize every single positive.
- Positives are universal while negatives are conditional.
- Downplay negatives as irrelevant, unavoidable, or

not impactful.
- Only address a few negatives, omit the others.
- Sound excited.

Option B (the opposition)
- Emphasize every single negative.
- Negatives are universal while positives are conditional.
- Downplay negatives as insignificant and irrelevant.
- Only address a few positives, omit the others.
- Sound reluctant.

After you perform this comparison, it should be a very easy choice for people.

People are generally lazy and don't like having to do their own research. When you control the conversation and actually address the positives and negatives of both sides, people will feel as if you've done their homework for them. You might not be 100% objective, but what's important is that you've saved them time. You've presented their choices to them on a silver platter, and more often than not, they will choose yours. By just sheer extreme comparison, it is easy for them to make a decision.

Framing different alternatives in a very vivid way has some pitfalls. If people sniff even for a second that you are being insincere, are attempting to be manipulative, or are over the top, you will lose all credibility. In fact people will assume that you lied and be against your Option A.

This is why it is very important when using this technique to never lie. You don't have to bend the truth to frame effectively because you should be creating arguments for and against issues. You can say the truth, but the way you position it in comparison to your proposal should still convince people and you will not come off as a liar.

Another best practice in framing is to illustrate the positives of Option A and the negatives of Option B. Illustrating can be anything from actual physical illustrations to colorful metaphors and analogies. If you can make a metaphor about (1) how big the difference is between the options, and (2) about something that impacts them emotionally (like their family), you will see a huge difference in compliance. For example, the difference between these options is like an Italian sports car and a tricycle in terms of speed and quality, or asking someone to imagine what they might choose for their children.

A final best practice in framing is to create emotional urgency. This is when you talk about how Option A will enhance someone's basic life needs, and how Option B will be a detriment to those same needs: security, physical harm, financial security, and relationships. For example, "Isn't this going to be much more effective for your health and weight loss?"

People want to run to pleasure and they want to run away from pain and loss. When you paint scenarios that threaten a sense of security, a sense of control, or even a sense of identity, people will react strongly. Dangling the fear of a huge drop in salary or the anticipation of a huge increase in free time will make someone decide instantly.

I cannot emphasize strongly enough the fact that you have

to always make people feel that they have a choice. You just want to make them hate one of the choices.

You have to make them feel that they have a choice because when you do this, it obscures the fact that you are stacking the information. It obscures the fact that you are reframing their choices in the direction you want them to go. But, do not give off signals that you are calling the shots for them or that they are going along with you.

The bottom line is that this is much better than lying. You did not twist facts. You did not make up facts. You did not pull fake statistics out of the thin blue air. Instead, you just laid out facts in such a way that the strong points of your solution shine the brightest and the negative aspects of alternative choices are front and center. It is really all about how you move facts around.

There's a final aspect of framing that will arguably make your option stand out more than anything else.

One of the most powerful ways to persuade people to do what you want them to do is to employ the principle of scarcity. Marketers do this all the time. Surely you've been to a website where there is some sort of timer counting down and warning you that you can only take advantage of a sale until the timer runs out. Also common are signs for 24-hour sales.

The marketers behind these promotions are tapping into a very powerful part of human psychology. We have a tough time turning down an offer that is not going to be around for long. The scarcity principle completely overrides the normal human tendency to be cautious and can make your position or opinion seem powerful and compelling.

You may be a generally logical and reasonable person, but the moment you see scarcity triggers like timers or 24-hour sales or one-time special deals, your self-restraint and self-control go out the window. You are no longer in control. Instead, you're focused on what you will be missing out on.

If the main character in *Life is Beautiful* had mentioned that his sole existing entrée was also a seasonal specialty, and the season was just about to end, that would be another factor in his favor.

Scarcity manipulates availability and creates temporal pressure. For example, you can persuade someone by saying that it's the last day of a sale, the stores are about to close, the manager only has a certain amount of time, and so on.

Framing is really a test of your imagination and creativity, but that is how persuasion works.

Statistically, you'll be facing poor odds or situations the majority of the time. You have to convince people to your side. If you went solely on the merits of a plan instead of the potential and persuasion that your Option A brings, you'd almost never win. Framing allows people to believe in *you* instead of in the hard aspects of a plan.

Chapter 11. Capitalize on Human Selfishness

One of the most common pieces of advice you'll hear about conversation is to get the other person to talk about themselves. The logic is that everyone is their own favorite topic, so if you get them talking about themselves, they will cherish the opportunity and talk your ear off (and they'll think the conversation was amazing). All you have to do is listen.

This highlights a basic human tendency that permeates all aspects of our lives. We always want to know, "What's in it for me?" and if the answer is something that pleases us, we care and become invested.

It's crucial to ask this question because it guarantees that we take care of our needs. You have to look out for number one because no one else will do it for you. They're all too busy taking care of their number one. If you want to not only stay alive but thrive, you have to ask yourself that question constantly.

Once you understand this core human trait, you have a tremendous weapon.

Because you know that people are self-interested, you can frame whatever it is you are trying to promote with that in mind. If you are going to go against their self-interest, you have your work cut out for you... so don't do that! Or at least make it seem as if you aren't. It's an uphill battle otherwise.

Instead of convincing people that your persuasive needs are important to them, why not directly appeal to *their* needs? If you frame the different benefits, features, and qualities of whatever solution you are promoting based on the prospect's self-interest, you will have a greater likelihood of convincing that person. Politicians know this and indeed are masters of it.

It sounds like a simple proposition, and it can be, but the problem that you will probably encounter is that people don't always like to be so transparent about what they want because it will make them feel selfish and judged by others.

For example, it's not often that you'll hear someone say "I want this restaurant because it's the closest to me, I'm lazy, and I don't care if you have to walk farther."

It doesn't matter if they are or aren't being selfish, but simply voicing their desires based on how they would benefit isn't something that people are willing to do.

This means that you will have to jump through certain hurdles to make your option, which clearly benefits them, socially acceptable. You have to make it safe for them to express that they want to benefit, and that's the tricky part in persuasion – guiding people to your choice without them knowing it.

This is why different people come up with types of cloaking mechanisms that allow them to pursue their interests but not appear to be doing so in a greedy or selfish way.

You have to work through that layer of wariness and guardedness that people have regarding their self-interest. In other words, you have to play the game of plausible deniability when presenting how an option benefits someone, so that they can plausibly have made their decision based on something other than just how much it fattens their wallet or stomach.

Always make it easy for people to say "yes" to something that benefits them by ensuring that they don't have to show all of their cards, so to speak.

You are the cloaking mechanism that allows people to capitalize on the self-interest that you are trying to persuade them to. In other words, whatever you trying to persuade someone to, you will be the factor that allows them to say yes to it without feeling like they will be selfish or judged.

For example, you might say that the restaurant has *your* favorite fish dish, or you really like the décor. That way if the person chooses that restaurant, they can frame it as if they are doing it for your benefit instead of their own. How thoughtful! It gives you plausible deniability.

This is a game because it is all about acknowledging and

working with self-interest in a socially polite way that will not be perceived as selfish by others. What do you think would happen to the world if everybody was blunt and obvious about their self-interests?

When you strip out all the niceties, we are all driven by raw self-interest. Human beings are driven by greed, lust, and the need for gain.

What selfish desires do people have that you can appeal to?

For example, if you are trying to get somebody to eat at a particular restaurant, the basic desire you can appeal to is their need to eat. But the problem is they can fill this need with many other options. You have to appeal to their higher, secondary desires and those things that motivate them.

Maybe socially connected people hang out in your restaurant. Maybe a lot of business deals take place in your restaurant. There are many different angles you can take and all of them address the other person's self-interest. Try to read the prospect you are trying to convert and pay attention to what their higher values are.

If this person is the creative type, maybe you'll want to play up the fact that your restaurant tends to attract a lot of artists and musicians. If this person is a business person, then you might want to tell this person that not only does the restaurant serve great food, but there are a lot of business organizations and networking groups that meet there and there are some business mixers that they might be interested in.

Pay attention to people and where they are coming from.

Once you can hone in on what is important to them, and what benefits they are seeking, you can use that as a guide for how you stack up your facts.

If you take a step back and look past all the accouterments that humans affix to their desires, you'll see that everything we do boils down to a basic human need.

Food, shelter, relationships, sex, entertainment, and security. We are always actively (and sometimes passively) searching for ways to improve our standing in those areas.

When you know who your audience is and what they want, you will be able to make a difficult choice very easy for them.

This stage is all about how your interactions with others impact your relationship with yourself. This is a very interesting level of maturity in terms of needs because it boils down to self-acceptance. You know you have a healthy level of self-esteem when you can accept yourself even if you are misunderstood or outright disliked by others.

For you to get to this stage and have a healthy level of self-esteem, you have to have accumulated certain achievements, or earned the respect of others. There is a strong interplay between how you get along with others and help others and how you feel about yourself.

The final stage is self-actualization.

The highest level of Maslow's hierarchy is self-actualization. This is when you are able to live for something higher than yourself and your needs. You feel that you need to connect with principles that require you to step beyond what is convenient and what is comfortable. This is the plane of morality, creativity, spontaneity, lack of prejudice, and acceptance of reality.

Self-actualization is placed at the top of the pyramid because this is the highest (and last) need people have. All the lower levels have to be met first before a person can reach this last level. You know you are working with somebody who operates at a truly high level when they do not focus so much on what is important to them, their self-esteem, or how other people perceive them.

This is the stage people are at when they say they want to find their calling and purpose in life.

They can focus on a project, idea, or concept that is way above their own petty self-centered concerns. These are people who can set aside their own needs and work for or toward something that is way beyond their mundane and self-serving concerns.

Sadly, many of us may never make it to this stage because we haven't fully satisfied the needs of the prior stages. It is a very privileged position to be in, and shouldn't be taken for granted.

Persuasion and the Hierarchy

How does the hierarchy fo needs relate to persuasion?

As I've stated before, the most persuasion is when you don't have to persuade at all, and this comes from understanding the people that you seek to persuade. If you can accurately pinpoint what needs someone may be lacking from Maslow's hierarchy of needs, then you can tailor your message to them differently or help them diagnose their mental blocks.

A lot of people that you meet are stuck at level one – physiological fulfillment. These are people who are just trying to get it together. They are all about survival. When they meet new people, it is all about whether those people can lead to better opportunities, security, or better resources. Frame your persuasive message in terms of fulfilling those needs and emotions.

Others might be having a difficult time because their

relationship and social needs aren't being fulfilled. So Maslow's hierarchy of needs gives us a framework to diagnose people in terms of what they are seeking. Essentially, it asks what concerns are preoccupying someone's mind, and what are not.

Can you ascertain whether someone is having issues with the following?
- Survival
- Security in accommodation and employment
- Personal and familial safety and health
- Relationships and friendships
- Romantic relationships and sexual intimacy
- Self-esteem and confidence
- Acceptance of self
- Self-actualization

If someone is struggling with one stage, then you know that they are also having trouble with the subsequent stages. It therefore makes no sense to appeal to those, because your efforts will fall on deaf ears.

Although no category of people can be said to be the easiest to lead, the stage that a person is in can push your persuasion objective to the bottom of their priority list. Someone is going to be less compliant and willing to compromise with you if they literally haven't eaten in days, or are struggling with depression, or have no friends.

You have to be aware of where people are in their needs hierarchy so you can tailor your message for it to actually be heard! Unfortunately, people are not going to tell you right off the bat. No one is going to volunteer this information. In many cases, you have to ask a lot of questions or possibly experience many things with them, so you can see how they behave in different sets of circumstances.

You have to put yourself in a position that allows you to truly understand where they are in the needs hierarchy, and recognize that their needs correspond to that level.

For example, if a person is in the safety or security level, that is their highest level of need. You can talk to them about love and belonging, self-esteem and self-actualization all you want, but none of that is going to register.

Some people are purely in survival mode. They are on the physiological stage and they are never going to leave that stage.

What is important is not to judge people based on where they are, but to position the project, concept, or product that you are trying to promote based on where they are on the needs hierarchy.

If you believe that everybody is prizing self-actualization, then you are sabotaging yourself because you will be sending the wrong signals. You are appealing to self-actualization when you should be appealing to physiological needs.

A major purpose of this chapter is to point out that people come to the table with different concerns in their life. Just because they outwardly appear to be on your level, you can't make assumptions about people.

In many ways, persuasion is like marketing – if you can help people with their pain points, then you've already won half the battle.

As I mentioned earlier, people are always looking out for number one. They are always asking, what's in it for me? In other words, they are focused on their needs.

This is why if you are able to address those needs in the form they want, you can be extremely

Chapter 13. Appeal to Ethos, Pathos and Logos

Don't let the Latin in the chapter title throw you off.

The ethos, pathos, and logos are, like other chapters in this book, a different framework to persuade people to your path. It is a framework developed by the Greek philosopher Aristotle, and in one form or another has been around for thousands of years. In other words, it's proven.

This method leverages the three most powerful motivations people have outside of themselves, the ethos, pathos, and logos.

Ethos refers to ethical concerns, pathos to emotional concerns, and logos to reason and logical concerns.

Ethos and ethics

An appeal to persuasion by ethos is when you attempt to persuade people on the strength of your character. The argument is that you are trustworthy and sound, and would never steer someone wrong. If your character is credible and trustworthy enough, then they have every reason to follow your lead.

"I've never steered you wrong in the past, have I?" or "I've done this a hundred times in the past, don't worry."

How do you make an argument about your character?

It usually comes from the past. Maybe you come from a good pedigree or you come from a very prestigious institution. You can also use your track record. Maybe you have shown that you are a fair and unbiased person who makes the right call every single time.

Maybe you've always carried yourself with dignity and class. The key takeaway here is that your power to convince the person you are trying to persuade revolves around your character. It can be your reputation.

Maybe you have shared experiences where people have seen you perform under pressure. They can see that you never lie. They can see that you never run away from a fight. They know for a fact that you always keep your promise.

Whether it comes from outside or from within, this method of persuasion is all about your character.

Appeals to character can only take you so far. Obviously, it does not work with people that do not really know you or with people with whom you do not really have a track record. It's limited, and depends on you to continually toot your own horn, which is a thin line to toe.

Pathos and emotion

Have you heard the word pathetic? How about sympathetic? How about antipathy? All these words share the same root, which is pathos. Pathos is emotion.

When you make an appeal to emotions, you are by definition not making a logical argument. You are depending on being able to take advantage of someone's emotional instability to win them over.

One of the best examples is displayed in Shakespeare's *Julius Caesar*.

Caesar, of course, was murdered on the steps of the Senate by a mob of senators who were sick of his reign. He was not without his supporters, who quickly came into danger by association.

Marc Antony, a supporter of Caesar, burst onto the scene and was able to masterfully play the emotions of the murderous mob. He made it clear that Caesar's supporters were there to bury him and not praise him, turning rage into sympathy. Logically it would have made sense to kill all of Caesar's supporters to ensure that his faction was completely destroyed, but once pity and compassion entered the equation, logic was long gone.

Marc Antony's speech is a powerful example of how an appeal to pathos and emotion works. You can either generate an emotional response in people to sway them, or you can capitalize on an existing emotional spike and harness it for your own purposes.

How do you make an argument that targets someone's emotions? By making them forget reality and logic. Use hyperbole and colorful, illustrative language that induces people to think outside the box of possibility. Craft emotional and intense stories to shortcut people's logic and engage their emotions. Make it personal to them, in a way that almost forces them to react in self-defense.

Above all, make them feel involved and affected.

Think about the television commercials that show sad looking dogs and cats in deplorable living conditions. They are the epitome of an appeal to emotions because they make you feel so personally involved that you act with a donation or adoption. These commercials are undoubtedly more effective than they would be if they simply stated the pros and cons adopting or donating to their organization.

More of our daily decisions are based on emotional triggers than we would like to admit.

Luckily, we are experts at justification and rationalization – we make an emotional decision, and then backtrack to rationalize it with reasons that may or may not be valid. We often let our emotions get the best of us, so we try to make it appear that we actually thought through our decisions.

Even if you feel your argument is dead in the water, you will be surprised how you can turn an otherwise slam-dunk case against you into a victory. That's the power of emotions – one of the most famous wars in (fictional) history began over a single woman, Helen, and her affections for two men. Is this logical? Of course not, but when honor and pride are in play, stakes can grow.

People don't always make decisions based on probability and the proper use of reason and logic. People are more emotional than they let on.

<u>Logos and logic</u>

Logos is when you try to convince an audience by using logic and reasoning.

Straight appeals to logic are very easy to see. You can see somebody appealing to your reasoning ability when they lay out an assertion and then support their assertion with facts. Truly brilliant argumentation breaks it down even further. They take the facts and then come up with different readings, either for or against their assertion, and then they knock down the objections raised by those facts.

There is a high degree of structure, and the argument almost reads like a debate.

An appeal to logos depends on the use of hard numbers and facts, and considers everything else speculative and non-determinative. Relevant comparisons are also used frequently.

All of the above is used to give the illusion that every piece of information has seen due diligence and is laid out in front. Logic dictates carefully analyzing the pros and cons, then making a decision based on them. Of course, this is a perfect place to use the situational framing we talked about earlier in this book.

An appeal to logos is what every other motivation attempts to pass itself off as. Some are obvious and transparent, but others are commonly mistaken and these are known as logical fallacies. For example, one of the most well known logical fallacies is an ad hominem argument, which disparages the holder of the stance instead of the merits of the stance itself.

They look as if they are making a sound argument by appealing to logic and reason, but in reality they are playing all sorts of tricks to prevent the audience from making a logical decision.

So which of ethos, pathos, and logos is best to appeal with? The answer is all of them at once, in a specific sequence. Human beings are emotional creatures and we have to be emotionally engaged – we have to *care*. The best forms of logical argument get the reader emotionally invested.

Therefore, the best use of ethos, pathos, and logos is to begin by appealing to emotion to draw people in and make them care. Emotions are the gateway. Next, frame the issue in a logical way that makes your argument bulletproof and infallible by dismissing the objections. Finally, your character is why people should listen to you and consider your words valid as a whole.

This is the basis of most sales and marketing, whether the salespeople and marketers realize it or not. These are the three basic human motivators, and by ensuring that you hit all three in a specific sequence, persuasion becomes more organized and inevitable.

Chapter 14. Subconscious Linguistics

It is very easy to get taken in by the hype surrounding the subconscious mind.

That's what we get for introducing people like Freud and hypnotists into popular culture.

The hype imagines the subconscious as a fertile playground for which there are all sorts of triggers that tap into subconscious actions and pathways. You just need to know what you say and when to say it, so you can tap into these subconscious habits and steer your audience members toward certain choices and away from others.

That is a myth, but there are aspects of scientifically validated truth there, especially with regard to triggers.

People do develop triggers. When they are exposed to these triggers, they tend to engage in routine action. The important part for us is that this plays out not in the form of physical actions, but verbal cues.

Triggers that those in positions of authority tend to use are what you should integrate into your vocabulary. In other words, there are certain ways of speaking and certain phrases to use to persuade people without them even realizing it.

They are manners of speaking and phrasing that assume leadership, authority, and performance of action. They access the subconscious in ways that cause it to skip preliminary steps like asking "Should I do this?" and go straight to "How and when should I do this?"

Enter the embedded command.

If a co-worker says, "Okay, so when are we having a meeting?" it assumes action first and foremost, and is phrased to take away your choice about whether or not to even have a meeting. It forces a positive response, which is far stronger than when someone asks "Do you want to have a meeting?" which allows people to refuse. In the first form, the person is asking the question in a polite yet commanding way. He is actually telling you to do something.

The second sentence places the action on you by asking you directly whether you want to have a meeting. In other words, you become the decision maker. You are the only person in the picture, and with that position comes a mental burden. You are not just deciding for yourself, but you are also deciding for another person or group friend. When you give people complete freedom, it is often paralyzing and makes them pause and think too much. When you use an embedded command, you are able to jumpstart them into taking action with a slight mental push.

This is a powerful technique because not only are you being commanded more forcefully by the first sentence, there is a bit of peer pressure there because the decision point is not just going to impact you, but other people too. This is why embedded commands work so well. They are subtle, but they trigger how you process information.

Another example of effective persuasive phrasing is restricting your audience's choices when you ask them a question. For example, when you ask "Red or white wine?" compared to "Would you like a drink?"

With the first question, it is already assumed that they are going to drink (and that they will be drinking wine). In other words, you knocked out all the other choices they might have had (not drinking, having a Coke or a gin and tonic, etc.). In the second sentence, you've given them a choice of whether to drink or not and what to drink. This triggers a broad range of options in their mind and you are less persuasive. If you are trying to persuade a person to drink, the first sentence will be far more effective.

Subconscious persuasion through phrasing can be extremely subtle. If people perceive a request versus a question, or one choice instead of two, they subconsciously relax their critical thinking processes and go with the flow. People are lazy, and people have busy days. This means that sometimes they just don't want the mental burden associated with the luxury of choice. Take advantage of this!

Another method to gain compliance and cement yourself as the authority is to use an embedded reward. For example,

"When we finish this next round of documents, do you want ice cream or tacos?" This question is pairing a reward with a sequence of behavior. For your employee to receive their reward, they must first finish more documents.

This technique is effective because it commands and assumes a sequence of actions. You are giving a choice of reward – tacos or ice cream – instead of the choice of more work. The sequence of actions and work itself are taken for granted and assumed. It can work like a charm.

Embedded cues take advantage of how the human psyche works and how we tend to program ourselves to respond to situations through habit.

Habits are self-preservation processes that allow us to go through daily life without running ourselves ragged with the mental strain of constant decisions. When we find familiar patterns in speech, for example, the brain works more efficiently and can rely on habit. If it knows that a certain outcome is almost guaranteed, then it will always tell your body to respond a certain way when it picks up certain cues from the environment. The human brain is a very efficient biological machine.

One research study trained rats to navigate a maze. Researchers tracked the brain activity of the mice as they navigated the maze. When the mice first began to explore the maze slowly, their charts would be exploding with activity and processes. It was all novel information to them, and they had to constantly make decisions and judgment calls.

But as the mice improved in navigating the maze, which never changed, their brain activity decreased. Researchers were shocked at how little activity there was once the habit was built.

The maze navigation study highlights the brain's need for efficiency. It does not like working on overtime, so when it identifies a shortcut, it will rely on that shortcut.

Subconscious leading and embedded statements take advantage of this proclivity to make canned decisions based on the signals that we see. This is another way that persuasion actually isn't about persuasion at all – it's about understanding people.

Here is a final way to use your phrasing powerfully – you can use it to make people invested and take ownership of something you want to persuade them to. For example, when you walk into a restaurant, what is the difference between "I've got a menu for you." versus "Would you like a menu?"

The first version isn't a question, it's a statement that assumes that you are invested already and that there's something specifically for you. It's tough to turn this away, even if you think that it's a persuasion technique. You never know if they actually grabbed it for you from a dusty shelf in the back. In other words, it makes you feel like you owe them a debt to take it, because they put in special effort to grab it for you.

The second version is a mere question, and it doesn't draw you in at all. There's no investment because it doesn't feel like the other person made an effort, so you have nothing to match.

The basic ways to use this type of phrasing to create ownership and investment are to imply that you are doing something specifically for them, or that you've taken an extra step, or to simply call them out specifically and say that it's for them so people can't hide in anonymity or invisibility and non-investment. You are pointing to a crowd and pulling someone out individually.

This phrasing technique to is essentially the opposite of the mob mentality and the bystander effect. The bystander effect is a psychological phenomenon which found that people in a crowd always believe that someone else will step up to take a necessary action, and that they don't feel obligation or duty because they can hide amongst the other bystanders. It was coined after an incident in New York where people walked by a woman being stabbed to death, and no one felt a huge duty to intervene because they all wanted the responsibility to lie on the other people in the vicinity, feeling none for themselves. Additional studies have shown that during emergency situations, you need to point to one specific person to call 911, otherwise everyone else will hide behind the bystander effect.

Chapter 15. Mental Strategies

This chapter talks about some quick and dirty strategies to boost your ability to persuade others. They're not quite as broad and overarching as the methods discussed in previous chapters, but they can still be very helpful depending on the context. Best of all, they are probably tactics that you've used before and never quite articulated. They will be familiar, but now they will be more replicable because you know exactly what they are.

But their simplicity can also be their flaw. Because they are quite straightforward, it might not take much to see right through them.

Promise of reward

One of the most straightforward ways to get people to do what you want them to do is to promise them a reward if they perform the desired action. Very straightforward and clear.

If you tell someone that in exchange for their support, you will reward them with something, there is a condition and a clear quid pro quo.

Among friends, you can offer people a ride if they go to the restaurant of your choice, or offer to buy them an appetizer. In the office, you can offer people your parking spot, lunch, to take over some of their duties, or give them credit on a project in exchange for going with your proposal. It can be a negotiation.

The key here is how subtle or direct you want to be about the rewards you are offering. The method you choose should vary according to how fearful of judgment the other person is. If they are more fearful of judgment, you can be subtler and not phrase it as a direct quid pro quo, but as a compromise, collaboration, or spontaneous idea of what you can reward them with. A more direct stance would be a direct bargain or barter.

This tactic is very easy to defeat, however, if the reward isn't strong enough or if the person is motivated by reasons other than personal gain. It's not as effective in a broad range of contexts because people are not always swayed by a transparent exchange, and often have a negative reaction to doing so. They want to feel as if they are making their own choice instead of being swayed so easily by a token gesture.

Promise of punishment

Of course, this persuasion technique is the exact opposite of the previous one.

When you use the promise of punishment, you tell them

that there will be negative consequences if they take the other course. You threaten them.

Again, this is the mirror opposite of the promise of reward strategy. In fact, it's such a mirror opposite that you can actually rephrase a reward and a promise as a punishment and a threat.

For example, "If you don't go with my proposal, it's possible that we won't get team lunches anymore." The best part is that it doesn't have to be a negative consequence that will actually occur, or that you will cause. You can promise all of the negative consequences as possibilities to avoid and warn against in your persuasion.

Keep in mind that there are two types of people. There are people who are proactive, and there are people who are reactive. The distinction also parallels people who take action to decrease pain versus those who take action to increase pleasure.

Proactive people are motivated primarily by what they stand to gain. These are people that dream big. These are people that tend to work toward goals. Reactive people often take action only when they think something, like their well-being and personal interest, is at stake. It's not until they feel that their backs are against the wall or that they might lose something that they take action.

This distinction between different types of people and motives is crucial to keep in mind. If you know you're dealing with a person who is prone toward being proactive, you might want to try the promise of reward method of persuasion. If you are dealing with somebody who is reactive, then you can try the promise of punishment method.

Keep in mind that most people tend to lean toward the reactive side. Most people only take action at the last minute when it's necessary. They will only act if they see that there will be loss, pain, or inconvenience if they don't.

A final point to keep in mind is that because this is a very direct and transparent technique, people may not comply with you because they don't want to appear to be afraid of your wrath.

Confusion

This is a psychological phenomenon known as "disrupt them reframe."

This was discovered by selling cards to bypassers. There were two ways that the cards were marketed:

"$3.00 for 8 cards"

Versus

"300 pennies for 8 cards (bargain!)"

Surprisingly, or not, the latter choice sold better.

Researchers theorized that it sold better because people's routine thought processes were interrupted and confused because of the way it was priced. That's the disruption.

The mind becomes busy interpreting that disruption of the odd manner of pricing and trying to reframe it into something familiar, and that's when you can strike with asking for the sale. There will be much less resistance because the brain is otherwise occupied by the disruption of the price.

Essentially, people are more persuadable when they are pre-occupied in a subtle way. What can you do with this information?

Ask people an unrelated question, and then attempt to persuade them on something you want. Give people something to tinker with in their hands, then persuade. Distract, then persuade. Persuade while watching television or listening to music.

You just want to create a scenario where you don't have people's full attention, so they will be much more likely to take you at face value.

Debt

Debt is similar to reciprocation, but the difference is that debt is a feeling of crushing guilt. You feel like you've taken advantage of someone, and you want to rectify that feeling.

For example, if you took time out of your schedule to help somebody with a task they were struggling with, they can become indebted or obligated to you.

If they know how important your time is, how busy you are,

they will realize that they are in your debt. You went out of your way and sacrificed your time to help them. It doesn't hurt if you imply all of the sacrifices that you've made as well, and how big of a deal it is to you that friends help friends.

Most people know that time is money, and if not money, value. For example, if you spent a lot of time helping a prospect make a choice, it's not uncommon for them to say: "Well, I've spent a lot of time with you on this. I think I owe you now." If you don't get

When someone performs something, even small for you, make it clear that you feel in their debt.

Moral appeal

People tend to have a certain view themselves. Regardless of where they come from and regardless of what they actually do, people tend to stick to whatever moral guidelines are.

You can succeed persuasively by appealing to their morality. You appeal to their subjective sense of fairness and their appreciation for the right thing to do in certain situations. In other words, once you know how people think and what their conception of just or right is, you can tailor your message to appeal to that.

For example, if you know that someone highly values honesty, "I thought you were a really honest person, my proposal is the most honest of them all!"

The most difficult part of this is to determine people's moral leanings. You can do this by asking questions that require them to assign values to certain traits or characteristics. However, when the chips are down and things are looking quite rough, you'd be surprised how quickly morals are thrown out the window.

Positive and negative self-feeling

This is when you tell people that if they decide a certain way, they will feel better or worse about themselves. You have to phrase this in such a way that you appeal to the prospect in two ways.

First, you tell them that they will feel good about themselves by taking a certain action. Second, they can also feel good about that particular decision knowing that they made the right move. You are sending out signals on two levels.

For example, "My proposal is going to make you feel so relieved!" or "That other guy's project depends on child labor and you're going to feel so guilty."

Remember, there are two types of people – proactive and reactive. Reactive people are more susceptible to appeals that threaten negative self-feelings. They want to avoid feeling poorly, so they are forced to take action. Of course, proactive people are more influenced by positive self-feelings because they actively seek to improve their lives.

Positive and negative altercasting

Positive altercasting is creating an avatar that is endowed with every positive trait that you can imagine, especially in regard to the field about which you want to convince someone. Highly ethical, intelligent, a pillar of society. Let's call him Dale.

You trot Dale out when you're trying to make a point with respect to your proposal. Dale, the amazing pillar of society, wholeheartedly agrees with you on your proposal. Dale, such a smart guy with amazing judgment, has endorsed you. Obviously, your proposal is sound and should be followed.

See how this works? You invoke this ideal, highly intelligent person and implicitly contrast him with your prospect.

"Gosh, Dale is such a pillar of society. He's the most moral guy I know! He also teaches a class on morality at the local community college, which is very cool."

You're indirectly applying pressure on your prospect. You're saying that anyone as moral as Dale would take your deal. If your prospect possesses any of Dale's positive traits, they will instantly go for the deal.

Negative altercasting is the opposite of positive altercasting. Instead of appealing to highly desirable traits and qualities like intelligence, morality, doing the right thing, ethics, and so on, you focus on an avatar's negative traits.

The avatar you conjure, let's call him Dan, has poor morals, judgment, and is overall a dim bulb. He's an idiot.

As you did with Dale, you invoke Dan to draw a contrast to your prospect. You indirectly tell your prospect that he's surely not like this imaginary person, is he?

"Only Dan would accept something so stupid, and Dan once went to the beach to surf the Internet." Anyone with an ounce of brains would do the opposite as Dan, and Dan is opposed to your proposal.

As with any kind of negative reinforcement, the key here is to get people to react. Get them to avoid being identified with a person who has negative traits so they make the decision you want them to make.

Altruism

Altruism is appealing to people's kindness, or the perception of kindness they have about themselves. An altruistic person is a do-gooder. A lot of people have an idealized view of themselves as good people, and being altruistic is usually part of the mix.

In Maslow's hierarchy of needs, concern for others and transcendence are at the top of the pyramid. Most people innately share that ideal.

When you appeal to altruism, you are appealing to people's highest needs. This may not be the level they're actually in, but it may produce enough feelings in them that you can persuade them to do what you want them to do.

For example, "Can you imagine how much the starving children will benefit from this project over that other project?" You invoke their sense of compassion and innate inclination to help others and make a positive impact.

Of course, you may find that many people make no pretense about being compassionate and kind, so this technique will work less often than you might think.

Exclusivity

Exclusivity is a persuasion technique used to make an option appear valuable, exclusive, and like a choice that only enlightened people would make. And of course, only high-level and evolved people choose it, so the person you are trying to convince should probably choose it and benefit from their exclusive knowledge.

Conversely, other choices are NOT high-level or intelligent, and you are just showing yourself as a primitive thinker if you choose those one of *those* options.

For example, "I know the other CEOs all chose this option, while the other option seemed to appeal to the secretaries more" or "Yeah, this proposal is definitely more nuanced and sophisticated, anyone with any training can see that."

Lead them to the light

This is a little bit different than talking about the positives and negatives of an option.

Leading them to the light means positioning your option or proposal as the solution to a problem and therefore a great relief of pressure and stress. The way you create this contrast is by leading them into a dark world that is the status quo. In a sense, you are actually creating a problem out of nothing so you can present your option and persuade them to choose it as the solution.

In other words, you make the current situation appear terrible, and you continue to agitate the problem. Take them into a dark place, and then present your proposal as the solution to lead them into the light. Sow seeds of doubt and fear.

For example, "It's terrible, isn't it? How that affects our daily work life. And the hours, and how we can't see our children as much. The money isn't nearly worth the hours spent. And I'm getting sick more often, aren't you? This proposal would help so much...."

Foot in the door

The foot in the door technique makes use of a compliance ladder.

A compliance ladder is a chain of events that starts with a person saying "Yes" to you in a simple way. Then, once you have your figurative foot in the door and their compliance, you keep upping the stakes until you work up to where you intended to be. The idea is that when people accept you once, they are then psychologically more open to each subsequent suggestion you make, even if what you are asking them to agree to keeps escalating.

For example, it's far easier to sell someone power windows and other bells and whistles in a car once they've yes to buying a car at all – there's an element of "why not?"

<u>Door in the face</u>

This technique may sound similar to the previous one, but it actually operates on the opposite theory. It doesn't depend on working your way slightly up, gaining trust slowly, and making your point in an escalating manner.

The door in the face is when you ask for something big knowing you will be turned down. But that's not the point – the point is that anything less you ask for after that will make you appear reasonable and proportionally gain more compliance.

For example, if you ask someone to pay you $10,000 for something, they might scoff at it. But when you immediately follow with $5,000, you have their attention because it seems much more reasonable.

Any of the quick and dirty persuasion techniques in this chapter can be used to tilt the scales in your favor!

Chapter 16. Underhanded Persuasion

The final chapter to this book on persuasion and taking advantage of human psychology has a decidedly different tone.

It's about attacks, insults, and ways to make a negative impact on people when you want to make a point. After all, we find ourselves in different situations on a daily basis, and though I am someone who teaches the opposite of the results that attacks and insults generate, it's also important to recognize what goes into a great, persuasive attack so you can defend yourself against them.

When you can understand these, and subsequently be able to see them in action against you, you will immediately be able to call them out. You won't have to wonder why you felt so negative after an encounter, and you'll know how to counteract it on the spot, to either crumble someone's persuasive argument, or elevate yours.

When I was a child, I was what you might generously call "husky." Euphemisms aside, I was one round child, and I was called all the names in the book. Arguably, the reason I have the semblance of a sense of humor is because I had to develop one as a defense mechanism. Whenever someone made an insult or jab at me and my weight, I would simply make a joke out of their statement, and in doing so, turn the laughter into a collaborative laughter instead of one directed solely towards me.

"I'm so fat that I have gravy in my veins instead of blood? Well, that's why your family likes having me around during dinner more than they like you."

And so on.

Simple, binary insults about a person are easy to deflect, amplify, or simply diffuse. They can even be formulaic to be transformed into something that will make people laugh with you as opposed to at you.

What about more nefarious tactics that can put you in a serious verbal or persuasive bind? It's not that you should approach each daily conversation as a potential wrestling match, but you don't want to be caught flat-footed when it does happen. Of course, if you're trying to persuade someone (or someone is trying to persuade you), negativity can often manifest.

I'm going to talk about a few of these tactics, how they work, how you can use them, and how you can defend against them.

The Double Bind

This is otherwise known as an intentional "between a rock

and a hard place."

A double bind situation is where someone is presented with two choices, but they actually lose if they choose either option. The person faced with this situation usually does not have the ability to change frames and create their own solution, so they must choose between options that are detrimental to them – and usually beneficial to the person who presented the choices.

Usually a situation like this is meticulously planned and crafted by someone that wants to be persuasive or attack effectively. It is even more effective if the trapped person is unaware that they are in a double bind and chooses what they think is a more beneficial option to them.

The way to use this as an attack on someone is to call out something you perceive them to be doing wrong in the moment and contrast that to another negative action. Already, there are only negative options.

For example, if you're trying to persuade someone of something, you might state, "You're not being logical. You need to look at the actual data I have instead of relying on your wild hunches."

In the face of such a statement, the other person has two options: agree with you and be more logical and act on the option, or remain illogical and refuse to look at any data.

If they choose the first option, they appear to be reacting and agreeing with you, thus subtly ceding control to you. "Oh, you're right, I need to look at the logical data." If they choose the second option, they remain illogical and appear close-minded, as well as ignorant in the face of a persuasive argument, "Nope, I won't look at the logical data."

Of course, there are additional options, such as the person refuting the validity of the data, or emphasizing the expertise upon which they based their hunches, but those aren't the options presented to them, and more often than not, people will choose from what's in front of them.

It doesn't matter what the response is. Either way, they come out looking weaker, like they agree and are in compliance with the persuader, even if it is subconscious.

Here's another example: If you're trying to persuade someone, you might state, "Can you please stop being so emotional about the decision? It's a clear choice if you remove emotion from it."

If they choose to act on the first option, they acknowledge that they are being emotional and that cedes control to you. If they choose to act on the second option, they are just being emotional, which is inherently viewed as an unbalanced way to make decisions.

Double binds are tricky ways you can assert control over others, and you can defend yourself by actively seeking third options. They present you two options that are both assumptions, and you must view them as such. Assumptions are not always true, proven, or even valid. Poke holes in the options themselves and don't let yourself feel confined to what is presented to you.

Praeteritio

As you may have guessed, this is a Latin term. What does it mean?

Praeteritio is a technique where you seem to appeal to a moral high ground, but you are secretly taking the dirty, low road. Essentially, it is when you bring up an insult or negative topic by stating that you won't be bringing it up. You mention something while simultaneously saying that it is not to be mentioned nor discussed.

It is persuasive irony.

For example, "I could mention when you stole from the cashier, but I won't do that. I wouldn't want to drag your name through the mud and take you through that again. You've suffered enough after you did that and took your punishment."

The key here is that you claim you will not be mentioning the incident because of a higher moral ground. Most of the time, the negative aspect mentioned is a direct attack on their actions or character.

It's difficult, and usually too transparent, to attack someone directly and explicitly, so praeteritio allows you to do so in a sneaky manner that prompts the other person to say "How did that negative aspect even come up?" You are able to say something direct while pretending that you weren't intending to, which invokes the wonders of plausible deniability. Plausible deniability, of course, is when you do something, but have a flimsy reason for doing it in a way that excuses you via negligence.

Another example would be, "I refuse to discuss your nefarious past and former prison record."

Praeteritio simply makes people feel bad with the reminder that you haven't forgotten about their past affairs, and puts them on the defensive subtly at the very beginning. This gives you a slight edge because they are diverting brainpower to defending themselves, instead of arguing against you or your persuasion.

Defense against praeteritio is to simply call it out as an obvious ploy. Once you can spot this in real life, you can disarm it fairly well simply by telling people what they are doing and characterizing it as manipulative.

Paralipsis

This is another Latin term that comes from the Greek word *paraleipein*, which means *to omit one side*.

Paralipsis is another sneaky persuasion and attack tactic that allows you to say something directly under the guise of being kind and morally elevated.

It sounds something like, "Let's focus on all the benefits, and not the cost or opposition to this project."

What just happened there?

An assertion was made to omit something, but in doing so, the topic is brought into the spotlight. It is phrased in a way that makes it impossible to ignore the negative nature or implications of the cost and opposition. It is a statement that at first glance sounds like it was supposed to be, "Hey, we're above this. Let's talk about the real things that matter" and turns it into, "Well, what about the cost and opposition to the project?"

It's the same phenomenon as when you say to not picture a yellow elephant on the page as you are reading this. What did you just picture bouncing along on top of the words? I'd wager that a yellow elephant just popped into your consciousness!

In stating that we will omit something, we draw attention to it. Here's another example: "Everything about him is great if you ignore his career." Once you've used that breadcrumb, it's impossible for people to not pursue it. You are almost begging for further engagement on the topic.

Defense against paralipsis is similar to defense against praeteritio. You must call out someone who uses this as transparently trying to instigate or insult you, while trying to hide their intentions. Once people are aware that you know what they are trying to accomplish, and that no one is being fooled by it, they will usually stop out of the guilt of being caught red-handed.

Do not let them hide behind obliviousness or plausible deniability. They know what they are doing and they are doing it in a slimy way.

The Straw Man

This is an argument tactic that you might be familiar with, but it's consistently popular (and hated) precisely because it still works on people, regardless of whether they recognize it or not.

The straw man tactic is a logical fallacy where you distort someone's argument, or defense into something that you can easily disarm or persuade against. People often do this without realizing it, and it still works.

For example, if someone tells you they disagree with you because something costs too much, then you might reply, "So you're saying the health of our country's youth has a price?"

In reality, that may not have been what they said at all, but you distorted their argument into something that you can universally disagree with. You are making it easy to persuade against them.

Think of it in this sequence.

1. You are presented with Argument A that you disagree with.
2. You distort or exaggerate Argument A into something that most people would disagree with: Argument B.
3. You attack Argument B.

Many people may not realize that you are not truly defending yourself against the actual topic that being discussed, but that's why it's important to carefully choose how you distort Argument A into Argument B. A more subtle way is to simply amplify the negative effects of

Argument A so that they could plausibly lead to Argument B in a chain of worst-case scenarios coming true.

When using this tactic, you are not lying or connecting unrelated concepts simply to disagree. You are making small leaps of faith that are actually related in many ways. It's plausible!

For example, if someone argues that student loans are positive for society, you might argue against it by saying, "They are good, but what happens when people start defaulting on their loans because of the poor economy in the next year? You end up with people that are in holes they can't pull themselves out of, and mass bankruptcies. Are you ready for that?"

If someone says that they don't want to do the dishes that day, you would reply, "Really? There are so many bugs in here, sometimes I feel like the kitchen is turning into a pigsty."

Defense against the straw man depends on knowing the specific argument or topic that you are discussing, and not allowing any type of distortion to occur. The key is to spot when someone comes back to you with Argument B instead of Argument A. That's when you know they're trying to avoid discussing the merits of Argument A and sneak something by you.

Chapter 17. How to Plant an Idea in Someone's Head

Most of what is presented in this book you might call "overt persuasion." You are directly trying to make an argument to win someone over, or you are framing the options to get them to act in a way that you want.

It is overt because you are directly influencing them in one way or another. For the vast majority of those tactics, you would be able to able to ask them if they thought you were trying to persuade them. They would be able to answer with a "Yes, I think so." You are both aware of it and trying to outmuscle each other.

Of course, the better you get at those overt tactics, the more covert they become. People will have trouble ascertaining what your true intentions are. However, that takes practice, so I want to take this chapter to go over some more subtle and downright invisible ways of ultimately getting what you want.

It's all about planting ideas in people's heads. This means that even though you are trying to persuade them to do something, they won't realize it since it will feel like they came up with the idea themselves.

At this point, we know enough about human nature that even if we recognize that someone has a good idea, we might not necessarily act upon it because we fear it will make us look gullible, or suggestible. In fact, we might do the opposite, even if hurts our interests just to maintain our perception of autonomy.

When someone feels like they have generated an idea by themselves, they have no barriers to acting upon it. In fact, their resolve is typically strengthened because they want to confirm and demonstrate how clever they can be.

Going from the back door and planting ideas in people's heads is important because it makes you opaque. In other words, people won't see how you affect them, and that means *you can keep doing it*. It seems insignificant, but think about it this way: if you want someone to buy more milk because you like milk, they'll buy more and more without realizing that it's for you. This is the best type of persuasion, because people will do things without prompting or convincing.

Embrace the Status Quo

This is one of the easiest ways to plant an idea in someone's head. Let's use the example throughout this chapter that you want someone to buy a car.

If you want to plant the idea of buying a car in someone's head, you're going to woefully embrace the status quo of not having a car, and all the pros and cons. Of course, you're not actually embracing of it, but that's how you present yourself externally.

The way to do this is to be happy and upbeat about the carless status quo in front of the person. Give the impression that a car is extraneous, overly luxurious, and plain unnecessary.

At the same time, drop in small statements about how much better life would be if you had that admittedly unnecessary luxury. You'll have to sell the benefits and pros, because that's what is going to make people imagine it for themselves. You're essentially thinking out loud with the benefits, but it is masked because you completely embrace the status quo.

"No, I love walking. I actually try to walk for twenty minutes every day because it keeps me active! Sure, it would be great to have a heater in the winter here, and maybe I wouldn't have to wake up early to wait for the bus, but hey! It builds character. I didn't grow up with a car, so what's the difference to me if I can get places quickly or not?"

See how disarming it is in the way that is phrased? It's indirect, there is no pressure, it's simply a way to talk about how great a car would be, while being externally fine with not having a car.

Accept the Status Quo

This sounds similar, but uses a different manner of phrasing to plant an idea in someone's head.

In the prior tactic, you appeared overjoyed to not have to deal with a car. In fact, it seemed like your preference. You talked about the benefits of not having a car, and the benefits of having a car. You kept it positive.

In this scenario, you are merely **accepting** the status quo. You don't prefer it, but you face too many barriers to successfully change it.

If we take the example from before, and you want to persuade someone to buy a car, it means you wish you could have a car, but maybe don't have the money yourself, or don't have the time to research your options. Then, because you merely *accept* the status quo, you will show your displeasure with the situation and bemoan all of the negative consequences that you will have to face as a result of those barriers.

Embracing the status quo seems positive, *accepting* the status quo goes negative.

"Yeah, we don't need a car. I guess we will just have to deal with the negative consequences of taking the bus everywhere, dealing with all the walking, and struggling when it's cold outside and raining. We'll figure out how to deal with everything as best we can."

Have you noticed that these objections are the exact same things that were previously spun as things you were *excited* to do and embrace?

Essentially, when you accept the status quo, you do so

bitterly and reluctantly, and hammer on how much worse your life will be. But, after all, you accept it, so it's not a message designed to convince anyone directly. You just want to get them thinking about what you've said without pressure to change the situation.

Talk *Around* the Idea

In other words, beating around the bush. Let's keep using the example of buying a car.

When you talk *around* the idea you want to persuade people to, you talk about adjacent tangents, you talk about the idea in general, and you talk about the benefits and the costs of the idea.

To talk around the idea of buying a car, you would talk about transportation, motorcycles, busses, commuting, how cheap a car would be, what kind of cars you like, and stories that involve cars. You're talking about the subject, but not the actual idea you want to persuade them to. You're telling stories involving the subject and idea.

You must be subtle here, otherwise it can easily become obvious that you are trying to manipulate someone.

Your overall goal here is to use an indirect tone, and simply broach the topic and continue to expose them to it. You want to deliver an eventual and slow epiphany to them. That's relatively easy when you act as if you have no preference, no stake, and you are just presenting facts and stories involving cars and transportation.

Once they are inundated with information and thoughts about cars, they are only a short step away from thinking "What if I buy a car?"

Play Dumb

As the name suggests, this is when you play dumb and ask the other person about a problem you have. You let the other person come up with the solution to your problems.

Your problems, of course, are most easily solved by someone purchasing a car. It doesn't matter that they are solving *your* problem for *you*, this merely allows the idea to take hold in their mind that a car can be the solution to many problems.

For example, you are having issues with being late for work, or you have back pain that makes it difficult for you to walk more than a few blocks at a time. Present this question to someone, and then ask them pointed questions about how you can solve the problem.

"How am I supposed to do that?"

"How can I get to work faster and not have to walk as much? I'm just so lost!"

Ask innocent questions to get the other person to brainstorm and come to that solution for you. Playing dumb can be deadly effective.

Planting ideas in people's heads is all about taking the back door and gently exposing people to your thoughts while hiding your intent. Covert works.

Chapter 18. The Anatomy of Hitler's Persuasion

Arguably, Adolf Hitler was one of the most persuasive people to ever walk the face of the earth.

What could he put on his persuasion resume?

For starters, he seized power within the Nazi party of 1930's Germany, and was subsequently able to convince millions of Germans that genocide was acceptable, if not necessary for Germany's continued survival. Along the way, he also convinced millions of Germans that they were on the cusp of creating a thousand-year-long empire, and that Germans were the most supreme and clean race of all human beings.

Whether or not people truly believed in these claims, they still acted upon them. What exactly was Adolf Hitler employing on a daily basis to make people follow his lead, despite his dubious claims?

A prevailing theme throughout this book you should have noticed by now is that people are persuaded by emotions and presentation. If all we looked at were hard data and facts, why would people ever come to different conclusions? There would be few ways to interpret the same data, and we would never have a problem with getting people to do what we want, as long as there was data to support it. More often than not, there would be a clear answer.

This is why learning persuasive techniques is so important. We're not on an even playing field where the data always dictates decisions. Hitler took full advantage of that, so let's look at a few of his major techniques. This chapter could be an entire book, and indeed books have been written about his persuasive influence, so I'll try to give an overview of his most effective methods.

False Dichotomy

Hitler created a very specific view for Germany and repeatedly expounded on it to the public. In his view, Germany had a rightful claim to world dominance, but it was constantly in danger of being usurped and stolen away.

When you create a strict view of anything, it means that people are either for you or against you. For example, "only bread is healthy" essentially means that ANY other food is unhealthy. It is then easy to say that "you must only eat bread or else you'll become obese" because of that strict definition. Your world becomes judgmental and pre-defined.

Of course, in reality that's not true, but that is the benefit of defining your objective in very specific terms. You can use black and white language to create "either/or" scenarios that don't hold up to scrutiny, but make sense if you take the specific view to be true.

This is called a false dichotomy: when you reduce a choice down to black and white two options, but you control how the options are created and thus control which option people choose.

For example, Hitler defined Germany as supreme, yet persecuted, as a result of World War I and the ensuing Treaty of Versailles, which greatly hamstrung German influence and power. He then created the false dichotomy that anything he suggested was to help Germany remain free and powerful: "We must segregate and intern Jewish people or else our race will suffer."

You can use this in two steps: one, by strictly defining your objective, and two, categorizing anything outside your option as negative. You create two choices, one of which leads to catastrophe – it's not much of a choice at all. For example, "We have to buy from this company, or we run the risk of going bankrupt."

He did this constantly and always phrased his actions to the benefit or downfall of Germany.

Create In-groups

Hitler's speeches took on very common, repetitive structures that were intentional in nature.

His first step was to frequently point out the commonalities of the German people and others that listened to him. He talked about what they shared, their common struggles and victories, and their national identity.

He cultivated a clear group identity full of triumph, positive emotions, and shared experiences. In doing this, he created a national pride and jingoism that also tended to create a feeling of superiority over other nations.

Above all else, by creating an in-group, Hitler created an "us versus everyone else" mentality.

You can do the same by very deliberately pointing out similarities between you and the person you are trying to persuade. That way, they will feel that they have similar values and mental processes, and that you have their best interests at heart.

You may also be able to take advantage of people's inherent laziness and desire to have decisions made for them. If everyone is the same as you, and they think this certain way, then you probably should as well.

Finally, Hitler and the Nazi Party recognized the power of the mob effect, social conformity, and groupthink. People are far more susceptible to emotional contagion and peer pressure in groups, so they created huge group events such as parades and festivals with mandatory attendance.

Amplify Negative Emotions

The next part of Hitler's speeches typically took the focus off of the German people and focused on negative emotions. Negative emotions are often the strongest motivators – specifically, the desire to avoid negative emotions.

Among others, he invoked feelings of rage, anger, righteousness, fear, inequity, and revenge. It hit everyone in the group the same way because he had created that in-group and found common ground.

Hitler led people down a dark road and painted a picture of how bleak the world currently was, and could be if there wasn't change. He made the status quo seem incredibly unjust and unhappy. He portrayed things in absolutes – massive injustice, the worst situations, and unbearable insults.

This would spark unrest and anger in someone, especially if they had been conditioned to believe that they were the supreme race above all others. With such unrest and anger in the status quo, the obvious place this would lead to was that action needed to be action. Change needs to occur as quickly as possible because the world is so bleak for this group.

And of course, this leads directly to the next step.

Provide Change

In the prior step, Hitler led his followers into the belief that the world was a dark, sinister place for Germans. To make it a lovely, safe world for Germans, change had to occur, and guess what?

Hitler positioned himself as *the man* to do that. He had the solutions, and they might be harsh, but they were necessary to creating a better world for Germans – and that was what was important. He was the agent of change to solve the problems for the German race, and the current world of bleakness and helplessness. He alone possessed the knowledge, willpower, and discipline to do it.

It's a very interesting sequence to follow and study, because once you arrive at the end, you have been led through a series of half-rational thoughts that, if taken to be true at face value, lead you to only one conclusion: Persuasion at it's finest.

Hitler and the Nazi Party were known to have studied Gustave Le Bon, who was a contemporary writer and researcher. Le Bon was known to have proposed that "ill-defined words" were the most persuasive and influential for their emotional responses and triggers.

Ill-defined words are those that are vague concepts that defy simple descriptions, such as justice, liberty, righteous, dominance, strength, and power. They are powerful precisely for that reason. People can't define them in traditional ways that universally agree, so they utilize mental shortcuts and attach a host of positive adjectives and emotions to them.

It's no wonder that when Hitler repeatedly hammered crowds with these ill-defined words, they hung onto his every word as their savior. They knew they wanted these words that were vague, yet overwhelmingly positive, so they saw Hitler as the key to action.

Conclusion

The world that my third grade teacher opened up to me was vast. She has influenced how I approach persuasion, and really, how I deal with people whenever I want to accomplish something.

Persuasion is the ability to have people follow you through whatever means possible, and the way you get to that point through artful human engineering.

It pays to realize that most situations you want to create in your life won't be a consensus. You will need to persuade people to give you a job, buy your house, go on a date with you, or closely examine your proposal.

Your daily objective is to take a group of people that will never be homogenous in opinion and figure out how to reach them.

People are driven by very different impulses. People are also affected by very different motivations, which means that you need to start playing persuasion on a higher, psychological level.

The great persuaders in history are tied together by two common threads: undoubtedly all had great charisma, but they all also had a remarkable understanding of how to appeal to people on their level.

Who knows, maybe my third grade teacher would have made a great politician!

Sincerely,

Patrick King
Social Interaction Specialist
www.PatrickKingConsulting.com

P.S. If you enjoyed this book, please don't be shy and drop me a line, leave a review, or both! I love reading feedback, and reviews are the lifeblood of Kindle books, so they are always welcome and greatly appreciated.

Other books by Patrick King include:

The Art of Witty Banter: Be Clever, Be Quick, Be Interesting – Create Captivating Conversation

Speaking and Coaching

Imagine going far beyond the contents of this book and dramatically improving the way you interact with the world and the relationships you'll build.

Are you interested in contacting Patrick for:

- A social skills workshop for your workplace
- Speaking engagements on the power of conversation and charisma
- Personalized social skills and conversation coaching

Patrick speaks around the world to help people improve their lives through the power of building relationships with improved social skills. He is a recognized industry expert, bestselling author, and speaker.

To invite Patrick to speak at your next event or to inquire about coaching, get in touch directly through his website's contact form at http://www.PatrickKingConsulting.com/contact, or contact him directly at Patrick@patrickkingconsulting.com.

Cheat Sheet

Chapter 1. The Butterfly Effect

The ability to persuade others and get them to follow you isn't just helpful and confined to employment or argument contexts. It's how you get anything you want life, because most of the things you want aren't handed to you. Persuasion skills run deep and are massively helpful in all walks of life.

Chapter 2. Understand Your Actual Audience

Your actual audience is the people that are on the fence in one way or another. Some people just can't be persuaded (by you), and that's okay. Don't focus on winning everyone – win who you can, such as people in the middle, sitting on the fence, who don't have enough information, and can clearly stand to benefit from what you are saying.

Chapter 3. Creating Emotional Debt

Emotional debt and the psychological phenomenon of

reciprocity is when you compel someone to act for or with you because they feel like they owe you. It can be big or small, but pointing out disparities or inequities can create emotional debt that makes people act against their own interests.

Chapter 4. Speak People's Languages (Communication Styles)

There are four distinct types of communication styles, and when you can pinpoint the styles that people tend to use, you can literally speak their language and be heard more easily. The four communication styles are: analytical, intuitive, personal, functional.

Chapter 5. Likability As Lubricant

This is an understated element of persuasion. If you are likable and charming, people will simply go along with what you say because they like you, don't want to let you down, and want to reciprocate the positive feelings that they have given to you. It is the ultimate lubricant because it isn't an argument in itself, it's just something that makes people react.

Chapter 6. Manufacturing External Credibility

External credibility, such as having graduated from a certain university, is something you might be objectively lacking, but there are ways of speaking and phrasing that can make you appear to be incredibly supported and validated.

Chapter 7. Elements of Persuasive Presentation

There are many elements of how you present your argument or proposal that can make or break your persuasiveness. Among them are the perceived accuracy of your argument, the perceived ease and simplicity, playing devil's advocate, and the perceived completeness so as to appear unbiased and painting an accurate picture.

Chapter 8. Exact Persuasive Phrases

There are particular phrases and words you can use to devastating effectiveness. If you can speak in absolutes, constantly allude to others, control the frame of a persuasive argument, and pepper in "ultimate terms," you will be well on your way to persuading people of anything.

Chapter 9. The Classic Challenge

This is one of the classic ways to persuade someone – an offhand challenge masked as the exact act you want someone to take. In other words, reverse psychology and using people's sense of pride, ego, and autonomy to your benefit.

Chapter 10. Constructing a Persuasive Frame

Persuasive framing is about how you characterize the options in front of someone. If you can marginalize the cons and maximize the pros, and vice versa for the opposing option, you can create a frame where there is only one plausible option.

Chapter 11. Capitalize on Human Selfishness

On some level, people are always thinking, "What's in it for me?" Take advantage of this and think about how you can characterize choices to people's benefits. Walk a mile in their shoes and think about their pains and triumphs.

Chapter 12. Utilize Mazlow's Hierarchy

Mazlow's hierarchy is a psychological model of what people need at any given time. Some people need food and shelter, while others are seeking self-actualization. It's incredibly useful for you to understand where people fall on the spectrum of needs so you can frame your persuasive argument to speak to them the most.

Chapter 13. Appeal to Ethos, Pathos and Logos

This is a Latin model of argumentation where you must be thorough and appeal to people's sense of logic, their sense of emotions, and their assessment of you as a worthy and reliable source of information.

Chapter 14. Subconscious Linguistics

There are ways of phrasing and speaking that make commands and suggestions subconscious to act upon. Typically, you are controlling the frame and giving people only choices that benefit you.

Chapter 15. Mental Strategies

This chapter encompasses a host of mental persuasion strategies to draw people to your side. These include:

promise of reward, promise of punishment, confusion, debt, exclusivity, altercasting, and leading people to the light.

Chapter 16. Underhanded Persuasion

This chapter talks about ways to be confrontational in an underhanded way, where people may not realize that you are accomplishing a goal at the same time. These include: the double bind, praeteritio, the straw man, and paralipsis.

Chapter 17. How to Plant an Idea in Someone's Head

Being covert and subtle about persuasion is always the goal, but that's difficult at first. This chapter talks about specific tactics to be hidden and secretive in planting ideas in people's heads. These include: talking around the idea, embracing the status quo, accepting the status quo, and playing dumb.

Chapter 18. The Anatomy of Hitler's Persuasion

Hitler was undoubtedly one of the most persuasive people of the century, and he did it through capitalizing on people's most powerful emotions of fear and anger. In doing so, he as able to rally a country to his cause and appoint himself as the agent of change because of how much fear and anger he made people see in the status quo.